Lillian Too
Jennifer Too

FORTUNE & FENG SHUI

HORSE

2021

KONSEPBOOKS
ASTROLOGY . FENG SHUI . INSPIRATIONS

Fortune & Feng Shui 2021 Horse

by *Lillian Too* and *Jennifer Too*
© 2021 Konsep Lagenda Sdn Bhd

Text © 2021 Lillian Too and Jennifer Too
Photographs and illustrations © Konsep Lagenda Sdn Bhd
Cover Art © Josh Yeo Zhu Lin

The moral right of the authors to be identified as authors of this book has been asserted.

Published by KONSEP LAGENDA SDN BHD (223 855)
Kuala Lumpur 59100 Malaysia

For more Konsep books, go to *www.lillian-too.com* or *www.wofs.com*
To report errors, please send a note to errors@konsepbooks.com
For general feedback, email feedback@konsepbooks.com

Notice of Liability
The information in this book is distributed on an "As Is" basis, without warranty. While every precaution has been taken in the preparation of the book, neither the author nor Konsep Lagenda shall have any liability to any person or entity with respect to any loss or damage caused or alleged to be caused directly or indirectly by the instructions contained in this book.

ISBN 978-967-329-299-8
Published in Malaysia, September 2020

HORSE 2021

BIRTH YEAR	WESTERN CALENDAR DATES	AGE	KUA NUMBER MALES	KUA NUMBER FEMALES
Metal Horse	3 Jan 1930 - 16 Feb 1931	91	7 West Group	8 West Group
Water Horse	15 Feb 1942 - 4 Feb 1943	79	4 East Group	2 West Group
Wood Horse	3 Feb 1954 - 23 Jan 1955	67	1 East Group	5/8 West Group
Fire Horse	21 Jan 1966 - 8 Feb 1967	55	7 West Group	8 West Group
Earth Horse	7 Feb 1978 - 27 Jan 1979	43	4 East Group	2 West Group
Metal Horse	27 Jan 1990 - 14 Feb 1991	31	1 East Group	5/8 West Group
Water Horse	12 Feb 2002 - 31 Jan 2003	19	7 West Group	8 West Group
Wood Horse	31 Jan 2014 - 18 Feb 2015	7	4 East Group	2 West Group

Cover Art by Josh Yeo Zhu Lin

Features a golden horse against a Van Gogh sky, paying tribute to one of the world's most loved artists. In 2021, the Horse may well be the luckiest of the 12 animal signs. This magnificent cover was painted first in the series, commemorating that fact.

CONTENTS

Chapter Three
FOUR PILLARS CHART 2021

Special Stars of 2021

Chapter Four
FLYING STARS OF 2021

Chapter Five
HORSE INTERACTING WITH OTHER SIGNS

Chapter Six
HORSE'S MONTHLY HOROSCOPE FOR 2021

Introduction to the Year 2021

Chapter 1

YEAR OF THE METAL OX

The coming year is the Year of the Metal Ox, a year when harvests are reaped as a result of old-fashioned hard work. It takes on the nature of the diligent Ox, whose finest qualities are its stability and steadfastness, the sign that symbolizes all the hard work that has to be done in order to prepare for the harvests and prosperity that follows. While the coming year can be prolific, there are few shortcuts to be had. Those who put in the hours and who match their effort with their wit will be those who reap the most from the year. This will not be a time for easy money or overnight speculative gains. It will be a year when substance wins out over panache, and when those who put emphasis on building solid foundations will prosper. One should strive to work first at what one can bring to the table, before making promises or trying to convince others of one's potential.

THE TOILING OX

This is the year of the Metal Ox, so it is one in which the Earth element of the Ox gets constantly exhausted by its heavenly stem of Metal. Earth produces Metal, so is exhausted by it. This is a year when the Ox has to constantly keep up its efforts to stay ahead. Individuals who are dedicated and disciplined will be the most effective and the most successful. The year can be an industrious one, but only if one acts industriously. There is good progress to be made for those who consciously and actively mirror the attributes of the steady Ox. It will be a year void of lightning speed success but conscientious work pays off. It is a year that rewards hard work over talent, where practice trumps winging it.

FORMIDABLE FRIENDS AND FOES

The Ox sign makes a loyal friend but also a formidable enemy, so the year will see both sides of this coin. Competitive pressures will be tough, but those with robust teams of collaborators and allies will succeed. Factions will form and there will be both poignant friendships and daunting foes. Those that stand alone will find it difficult to navigate through the various obstacles that the year offers up.

The Paht Chee of 2021 features both a troublesome clash and a promising alliance in its earthly branch line up. There is a clash between the Ox and the Sheep in the Day Pillar, but also an encouraging connection between the Ox and the Rat in the Hour Pillar. It is a year when friendships matter, so one must work at keeping one's friends. Those that slip the net to the other side could become intimidating enemies. People will tend to hold grudges and have long memories. The advice is to avoid offending the wrong people with careless words and unthinking actions. Skins are thin and offense is taken at the smallest acts of offhandedness.

THE LEADER REIGNS SUPREME

The twelve months from February 4th 2021 to February 4th 2022 will support people in leadership positions. Those who have recently risen to high office or who were promoted last year, whether in Government or in Commerce, will feel the benefits of the year's energies. Such individuals enjoy the buoyancy of the winds and waters that translate into a powerful flow of auspicious heaven luck. They benefit from a special vitality that aids their decision-making. Their actions carry weight and they find it easy to garner support for what they want to do.

PAHT CHEE CHART 2021			
HOUR	DAY	MONTH	YEAR
壬	癸	庚	辛
Yang water	Yin Water	Yang Metal	Yin Metal
壬子	己未	甲寅	己丑
Yang water Rat	Yin Earth Sheep	Yang Wood Tiger	Yin Earth Ox

With the #6 Heaven Star taking center stage in the year's Flying Star chart, leaders and those in positions of power are blessed with the mantle of heaven. It instills in them great authority and effect over their charges so they will have greater ability to influence the outcome of what they are engaged in.

This year favours leaders, chiefs, bosses, managers and directors of all kinds, and in all fields.

The danger this year is that the #7 afflictive star has arrived in the NW, the sector that represents the Patriarch. With leaders so powerful and with the treacherous #7 star in its home location, this brings the risk that those in power may use their position for harm rather than for good. Leaders with strong moral ethics can effect very positive change with a big and lasting impact, but those who act on a whim could end up making disastrous decisions that affect the fortunes of many.

The presence of the Ox-Sheep clash in the chart suggests that while leaders may be powerful within their own spheres, they meet with hostility from opposing interest groups, and leaders of other nations and organizations. Different blocs will have differing agendas, and when compromises cannot be reached, there will be conflict and struggle.

On the world stage, the influence of the #7 on the leader suggests there will be much fighting energy, and even risk of war. US-China trade relations will continue to deteriorate, with effects impacting more and more nations. Worrying alliances may be formed. There will be unified groups but it will not be one unified assembly; there will be powerful diverse groups that clash and clatter.

Conspiracy theorists may well have some premise to their conjectures; this becomes ever more likely if the ominous influence of the excessive Metal in the year's chart is not strongly suppressed. All may not be what it seems to be on the surface.

THE INFLUENCE OF THE ELEMENTS

 METAL *represents authority*
METAL in 2021 stands for RESOURCES, but it also stands for AUTHORITY.
Unfortunately, in 2021, authority may not always be benevolent. This year there is almost too much Metal energy, and too much makes the ominous side of this element stronger. Leaders become more powerful, and power here has to potential to corrupt. Checks and balances become more important, as the year could produce leaders who make unscrupulous decisions, taking into account only their own personal agendas.

This affliction affects not just leaders on the world stage but those in one's immediate sphere as well – bosses, community leaders, mentors, teachers, parents. If this Metal energy is not kept under control, it could lead to disastrous consequences in one's personal daily life. The effects of this can feel very real and close to home.

WHAT TO DO: We suggest displaying a **red-faced Kuan Kung**, the powerful Warrior God in the home and office to protect against the excess of Metal element energy. Having this God of War and God of Wealth in the home ensures you stay on the winning side of the element luck effect. Kuan Kung will ensure you make judicious decisions that end up benefiting you and your family in the long run. Gives you courage to move forward but tempers any misplaced bravado.

Red-faced
Kuan Kung with
5 victory flags

2. Wearing jewellery in precious Metals fashioned as sacred syllables and symbols transforms the effect of Metal from autocratic to benevolent. It helps keep you protected from harm and ensures you do not

lose the support of the people who matter most to your prospects in life- eg. Your boss, your parents, your teachers.

WATER *represents competition*
WATER in 2021 stands for FRIENDS and FOES, which are present in equal measure. Both have an equivalent part to play in the outcomes that follow. Because the year is one of STRONG WATER, the element of Water this year needs to be treated with caution. Too much of it could tip the scales over, attracting fierce rivalry and underhand tactics by one's competition, rather than cultivating strong allies that stay loyal.

This year it becomes especially important to carry protective amulets that guard against betrayal and disloyalty. Carrying an image of **Kuan Kung with**

Anti-Betrayal Amulet will help protect against becoming a victim of these energies. Always give others suitable respect, and don't disregard the dangers of allies changing sides. If the incentive becomes attractive enough, they will. Don't take anything too personally if you can adopt the stoic outlook of the Ox where you make the most of the opportunities open to you without complaining too much what is fair or not fair. You can effectively buffer against many of the pitfalls of the year.

THE COLOR BLUE – Blacks and blues stand for Water energy. While water to the Chinese traditionally represents money, this year it also signifies competition. Using too much of this color this year holds the danger of fueling rivalry and competitiveness amongst one's peers. Do not don too much black, and when you do, try to add a splash of color to neutralize its more sinister effects. Place the **Celestial Water Dragon** in the home to keep this element under control.

FIRE *brings wealth*

FIRE in 2021 stands for WEALTH LUCK. This is the element that appears to be completely missing from the year's chart and thus is the one we must actively work at replacing. There is hidden wealth brought by the Tiger, but this needs a trigger for it to be actualized. We suggest wearing the color red in free abandon this year. Remember, this is the Year of the Ox, an Earth sign whose inner vitality gets spurred on by the wonderful energy of Fire.

THE COLOR RED - Red to the Chinese is always considered lucky. It is a color of celebration and carnival. It is traditionally used in all auspicious occasions, and as we move into the new year of 2021, it is especially important to wear plenty of red! For the first 15 days of the Lunar New Year, we recommend getting yourself a red outfit for each day. Keep up this ritual through the entire 15 days of celebrations to ensure its effects can get you through the year. This is an excellent way to "fuel up" for the year, as it is a year when the element of Fire is glaringly missing.

In the home, keep the lights bright throughout the year. Change your lightbulbs whenever they start to flicker or lose energy, and don't try to save on the electricity bill by constantly turning off the lights! It is far more important to work at keeping this element properly energized through the year. Don't be penny wise and pound foolish. Lights represent Fire energy, and Fire energy represents wealth and prosperity in 2021.

NEW WEALTH WALLET: Each year it is an extremely lucky ritual to get yourself a new wallet and transfer some money from your old wallet over to your new one, while adding in some brand new notes

For Wealth

(best if from cash received as a Chinese New Year ang pow, or from one's latest drawn salary or bonus). You can also keep an image of the **Wealth God Sitting on a Tiger** in the form of a Gold Card inside your wallet; very auspicious as the Tiger is the sign that brings hidden wealth to the year.

Each year we design a wallet to vibrate and sync with the energies of the year, and for 2021, our wealth wallet features the stock market bull. It is the Year of the Ox and the Wall Street Bull is a most auspicious symbolic cousin of the sign of the year. The Wall Street Bull represents your investments going up, and your asset wealth growing.

We also have the **Asset Wealth Bull with Wealth Amulet** which will attract wealth-generating luck to any home which invites it in. Display prominently in the West where the *Star of Current Prosperity* has flown to this year or on your desk in front of you where you work. The idea is to see it daily and its subliminal effects will magically influence your actions and ability to attract wealth luck into your life.

WOOD *brings growth*

WOOD is the element that stands for growth. In 2021, it also signifies intelligence and creativity. It is what brings fresh new ideas to the mix, encouraging a blossoming of imagination and ingenuity. As we foray further into the new decade, old ideas will increasingly lose appeal and old technologies become obsolete with increasing speed. These need to be replaced and they will, and it will be those who can dream up the new ideas, methods, designs and technologies that will profit.

For the individual looking at making it in a rapidly changing world, it will be enhanced creativity and thinking outside the box that will help you. Surround yourself with the vibrant energy of plants and greenery, invite fresh flowers displayed in auspicious vases into your living space. If you live in a modern skyscraper city where feasting on green is difficult or unusual, look for ways to introduce indoor gardens into your home and office space, take regular time to visit parks and gardens, or make time to visit the countryside to refuel and recharge your senses with the power of nature.

THE COLOR GREEN – Greens of all kinds represent innovation and vision in 2021. Fill your wardrobe with lots of this color in emerald green, lime green, neon green, shamrock, chartreuse, sage, seafoam… all

of these will inject your wardrobe with
a fresh dash of inspiration and will
attract wonderfully inspired energies
into your aura. Green this year is very
lucky and brings to the wearer a new
lease of life. If you have been feeling
dull, uninspired or at a crossroads,
introducing a pop of bright green into
what you wear or carry will give you the boost
you need to change track, get moving, get started. It
is the "energizing" colour of the year and should be
made use of liberally and profusely.

TEND TO YOUR GARDEN: There's nothing that
invokes better yang Wood energy than thriving plants
and greenery. Make a trip to your local nursery and
bring home some vibrant new plants to add to your
garden. If you live in an apartment, introduce some
live potted plants into your living space. This will stir
up the creative juices in you needed to dream up new
ideas and to hatch ingenious strategies for your work
and in your life.

EARTH *brings power & influence*
EARTH in the Year of the Ox is the
intrinsic element of the animal sign of
the year. It is the element that symbolizes
stability, strength and permanence. It is the element
that ensures that however crazy the energy gets,
however quickly the world changes around us, we

can dig our heels deep and stay grounded with our values and our visions intact. Earth energy will prevent us being light-eared and light-headed, or easily influenced. In 2021, the element of EARTH also signifies recognition and power. It brings the luck of rank and position, and boosts one's chances when it comes to promotion and upward mobility, whether in one's career or in any climb to the top of any organization. Earth energy brings you influence and command and will make people listen to you.

EARTH COLORS – Wearing shades of earth tones brings you respect and makes people listen to you. It keeps you rational and well-balanced and envelops you with an aura of dependability. An excellent color group to use when you need others to take you seriously. Earth colors include yellow, orange, beige and cream, in all their shades. Wear such colors when you feel you need others to take notice of you, when you want to boost your influence over others and when you need people to listen to you. Those of you ambitious for your career to get a boost will benefit greatly from making use of earth colors.

THE 24 MOUNTAINS CHART OF 2021

The compass wheel around which the animals are positioned contain 24 mountains, which attract different stars each year. The overall fortunes of the year get enhanced or disabled depending on which

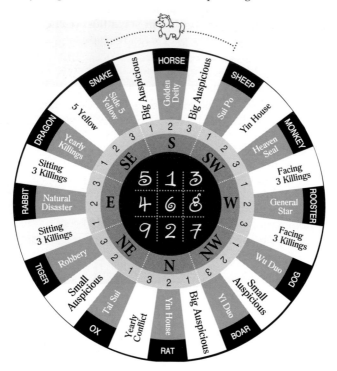

stars settle into which corners. Some years will have more auspicious stars, and some less, and their positions around the wheel impact on each animal sign differently.

THE LUCK OF BIG & SMALL AUSPICIOUS

One of the luckiest indications from this chart are the Big and Small Auspicious Stars, and in 2021, we have 5 of such stars making an appearance. The year enjoys three *Big Auspicious* stars and two *Small Auspicious* stars. The animal signs that benefit from these are the **Horse, Snake, Sheep, Rat, Boar,** the **Dog, Ox** and **Tiger**. The locations of these stars are spread out giving the above animal signs the potential to seize opportunities that come their way.

The sign that benefits most from this indication is the **HORSE**. The Horse enjoys two Big Auspicious stars, which suggests that after two difficult years, this sign is ready to take flight. The free-spirited Horse person can finally seize what it has been grappling after; this is a year when this sign can take risks and put wholehearted effort behind their passions. It is a year when the Horse should not rest on its laurels, because the big time has arrived.

The other signs enjoying Big Auspicious are the **Snake** and **Sheep**, and the **Rat** and **Boar**. These signs also have the potential to go after big dreams and, to

realize big ambitions they may have been harboring. For these signs, opportunities will be plentiful. Success comes for those who are hungry and resolute. Remember that this year, results do not come immediately, so one must not get discouraged if the path to actualization seems long or even impossible. The winners will be those with the staying power to keep at it and stay the course. Hold on to your dreams, and don't change your mind at every setback. Trust in your instincts and passions, and don't give power to those who disturb your mind or pour cold water on your ideas.

While the Stars of Big Auspicious bring really fabulous blessings, so do the Stars of Small Auspicious. These have the same effect as their big brother stars, but they bring success in smaller measures and in stages. The signs enjoying Small Auspicious this year are the **Ox**, **Tiger**, **Dog** and **Boar.** For these signs, they are likely

to meet with small successes that form the stepping stones to bigger success later on. For these signs, this is a year for building firm foundations and laying out the pathway for future triumphs.

Small Auspicious brings end goals that hold slightly longer time trajectories, but accompanied with the same staying power, success does ultimately come. Learn to celebrate the smallet of wins and stay clearheaded about your ultimate goals. If you constantly step back to examine the bigger picture, you will not lose sight of why you are doing what you're doing.

ENHANCER: Remember that *Stars of Big and Small Auspicious* bring the potential of great fortune, but to enjoy their benefits to the fullest, they need to be enhanced. Each year then, we design a Big Auspicious Enhancer to kickstart the very positive effects of these stars. This year, all animal signs benefit from displaying the **Six Birds Auspicious Multiplier**. This activator featuring an I-Ching coin with six birds and the auspicious amulet enhancer brings new opportunities. The 6 birds activates the #6 Heaven Star that rules the year's Lo Shu chart. The number 6 is the number of the heavens, which unlocks the celestial hand of the Gods. Display this potent activator in a place where you can see it often – either in a prominent place in the home, or in front of you on your work desk.

6 Birds Auspicious Multiplier. Unlocks the Big Auspicious luck of the year.

LUCK FROM THE HEAVENS

Two stars that further magnify the luck of the heavens are the *Golden Deity Star* and the *Star of the Heavenly Seal*. These land in the location of the **Horse** and the **Monkey**, bringing these two signs the luck of celestial fortunes. For these two signs, help comes without having to seek it. They enjoy the patronage of powerful mentors with many wishing to help them. They also have better instincts and can trust their own judgment more. For the Horse, as it also enjoys two Big Auspicious stars, little can go wrong as long as it stays judicious and diligent. The Monkey however needs to employ its trademark cunning to make the most of the Heaven Seal; it has to dodge the Yin House and Facing 3 Killings, but its main 24 Mountain star influence is extremely positive.

To make the most of these stars, we recommend that the Horse and Monkey invite in a **Golden Deity** into the home. Any Buddha, God or holy figure in line with your own faith will work. We particularly love **Kuan Yin, the Goddess of Mercy**, revered by Chinese all around the world. She is the female personification of the compassionate Buddha and brings wealth, health and happiness and protection from harm.

Kuan Yin

THE GENERAL STAR

The **Rooster** enjoys the General Star, which brings it power and authority, but unfortunately also fuels its short fuse and hot temper. But the Rooster this year has the very lucky #8 star, which enhances its fortunes and intrinsic energy. The Rooster as a sign does not suffer fool's gladly, so all these indications point to a Rooster that reigns supreme in 2021, but one who may be insufferable to those it considers "beneath" them, whether in intelligence or in status. To make the most of this star, all Roosters this year benefit from displaying the **Power Ru Yi**, the scepter of authority which boosts its command as boss or leader, while ensuring no disgruntled subordinates try to make trouble, or rivals rise up to try to displace it.

Star of the Yin House

This star brings danger of sickness and disease, and a general lack of energy to those it afflicts. It is particularly dangerous if one is already ill or elderly, or with other heavy afflictions indicated in their charts. This year, there are two Yin House stars and these arrive in the SW and North, affecting the **Sheep**, **Monkey** and **Rat**. All three of these signs are advised to take more care this year when it comes to health, well-being and safety. We strongly suggest that these signs carry protective amulets to shield them from the influence of malevolent spirits that may wreak havoc in their lives. Any of the **seed syllables Om, Ah or**

OM   AH   HUM

Hum will invoke the presence of the mighty Buddha, establishing a firm spiritual circumference of protection around the wearer.

If ill health is of particular concern, we recommend wearing and displaying health amulets. The **Wu Lou**, **Garuda Bird**, and the **Healing Deer**, bring precious cosmic protection. The deer is especially wonderful; this animal has always been associated with health, strength and vigor. It is also the animal that holds the solution to good health when all other methods have not seemed to work. There are many folk legends associated with the deer in all cultures, but in Chinese mythology, the deer is almost always shown accompanying Sau, the divine God of Longevity.

Healing Deer

The Robbery Star

This star brings money loss and betrayal and especially affects the **Tiger** in 2021. Those born under this sign need to be especially mindful not to get taken in by con men and getting cheated by others. There is higher chance of getting conned into undertaking bad investments. Business partners and associates could prove untrustworthy. It is also very important whenever one has this affliction to take care of personal safety. Robberies, muggings, petty thieves and street crime become more of a danger. This star also brings risk of becoming a victim of chance or collateral damage in somebody else's fight.

To counter this negative star, you need the image of the **Blue Rhino and Elephant** in the home, and you MUST carry the **Anti Robbery Amulet**. This protects against losing money and possessions. It is also important to protect against personal harm and injury; wear protective amulet at all times! Females in particular should avoid venturing out alone late at night or putting themselves under unnecessary risk; they should carry the **Nightspot Protection Amulet** for protection against petty crime.

Yearly Conflict & Yearly Killings

These stars bring obstacles to everything you do, making it difficult to make meaningful progress. These are the stars that can discourage you from remaining steadfast and keeping on your intended path. It throws up unexpected snags and hitches, and when left unchecked, can overwhelm one with feelings of depression and anxiety. These are negative stars that gather the slings and arrows of misfortune hurling them your way with some measure of ferocity. It is as such extremely important to take note of their location each year and take definite steps to neutralize them.

In 2021, the Yearly Killings star has landed in the **Dragon**'s location of SE1, and the Yearly Conflict Star visits the N3 sector, affecting the animal signs of **Rat** and **Ox**.

The *Yearly Killings Star* is deadlier and needs immediate action – we suggest that all Dragon-born and all those whose bedrooms or main door location are in the SE carry the **28 Hums Protection Wheel** and invite in the **Buddha image of Nangsi Zilnon Guru Rinpoche**. He is the warrior Buddha who completely overcomes all types of obstacles brought by the Yearly Killings.

28 Hums
Protection
Wheel

The *Yearly Conflict Star* makes everyone want to fight with you, bringing opposition to your ideas and making it difficult to see your projects through. Working in teams becomes especially difficult. At work, this could mean difficult colleagues and fierce politicking by workplace rivals. Those afflicted by this star could find themselves spending the better part of their time dodging potshots rather than focusing on their work. It makes work life very unpleasant, and the effects of this star can also permeate one's social and private life. This negative star arrives in the N3 sector affecting all whose main door or bedroom or office are located in this part of the home or office, and it affects Rat and Ox born people. Those affected by this affliction need to carry protection amulets and display the relevant cures. The **Dorje Drolo Scorpion Amulet** is especially helpful in this regard.

Natural Disaster Star

This star arrives in the East sector, affecting those who spend much time in this part of the home. This is the star that puts in you in harm's way – being at the wrong place at the wrong time. It brings all manner of natural misfortune including floods, fires, earthquakes, tsunamis, viruses and disease. If you are afflicted by this star, you MUST carry spiritual protection. ALL East-facing homes benefit from inviting in a statue of

 Guru Rinpoche, and all living in East-facing houses should wear the **Bhrum Pendant** which protects against all kinds of harm, illness, accidents and avoidable misfortune.

LUCK OF THE 12 ANIMAL SIGNS

Every animal sign is affected by a host of factors which change each year, producing a different basket of combinations which influence each individual sign's luck differently. Aside from the animal sign year you were born under, there are additional factors affecting your luck, but viewed together with these indications, anyone can alter the course of their lives and make intelligent decisions to maximize luck through any given year.

Here we summarize the broad outlook for the different animal signs, and in later chapters of this book, we go into greater depth and detail on what all of this means for you personally, depending on your heavenly stem, your home direction, your lunar mansion and your compatibilities.

The **HORSE** is blessed with extremely fortunate indications with the double *stars of Big Auspicious* and the *Star of Golden Deity* brought by the 24 Mountains Compass of 2021. This sign has great good fortune coming, which should more than make up for the unfortunate stars it had to endure in the last two years. The Horse is an energetic and restless sign full of passion and appetite for adventure, but the last couple of years will have made it difficult for it to pursue its desires. This year changes all of this; the Horse person will feel like a cloud has lifted, and as the year progresses, things get better and better. There are no unlucky indications at all, and the Victory Star #1 promises some very exciting new developments in the Horse's life.

The Horse should boost its fortunes with the **6 Birds Auspicious Multiplier** and benefits from displaying the **Desktop Flag of Victory** in its vicinity.

Desktop Flag of Victory

The **MONKEY** and **ROOSTER** are the signs enjoying the luckiest element luck indications. These two Metal signs have superlative Life Force and Spirit Essence, suggesting an inner determination that is unwavering. These signs know exactly what it is they want and how to go about getting it. Both Monkey and Rooster are known for their innate intelligence and ingenuity, and their already immense brainpower gets a big boost this year. The Monkey in particular enjoys very promising "success" luck; not only can it get what it wants, it receives plenty of recognition to go along with it too!

The **Rooster** can boost success luck by surrounding itself with the presence of the **Victorious Windhorse Carrying a Jewel**, as can the Monkey. Both these signs also have excellent indications from the 24 Mountains, with Monkey enjoying the *Heaven Seal* and Rooster benefitting from the *General Star*. The Monkey should carry the **Dragon Heavenly Seal Amulet** and the Rooster needs the **Ru Yi**.

Dragon
Heavenly Seal
Amulet

The sign that gets hit by the *Five Yellow* this year are the **DRAGON** and **SNAKE**. This indicates that these signs need to watch that the *wu wang* does not bring misfortune their way. The Five Yellow of 2021 sits in a Wood sector, which suggests it is NOT a deadly Five Yellow; nevertheless, the obstacles it brings can cause life to feel very unpleasant indeed and it should be strongly subdued.

 Dragon and Snake this year need to carry the **Five Element Pagoda Amulet with Tree of Life** to combat the afflictive energy, turning obstacles into productive challenges, and transforming unfortunate outcomes into promising ones. Both Dragon and Snake are signs that thrive in adversity, gaining strength and shrewdness when the going gets tough. And the *wu wang* of this year can be metamorphosed into positive rather than negative results. The Snake should have the **6 Birds Auspicious Multiplier**, while the Dragon needs the **28 Hums Protection Wheel**.

The WOOD ELEMENT SIGNS of **TIGER** and **RABBIT** both enjoy very good element indications but need to boost success luck with the **Victorious Windhorse** this year. The Tiger benefits from the *Small Auspicious*, and direct access to the hidden wealth of the year, but the Rabbit needs to do more work to boost its prosperity potential. The Tiger should display the **6 Birds Auspicious Multiplier** while the Rabbit MUST carry the **Three Celestial Shields Amulet** to stay protected against the 3 Killings affliction that affects it this year.

The WATER ELEMENT SIGNS of **RAT** and **BOAR** are the most unfortunate in terms of element luck, facing very bad life force and spirit essence. This can cause a sudden lack of confidence in one's own abilities and make these two signs prone to being easily discouraged. What the Rat and Boar need this year are strong cures to lift their inner energies. They need to carry the **Life Force Amulet** and **"Om" Dakini Spirit Enhancing Amulet**. What these two signs do have however are a shared *Big Auspicious Star*. Rat and Boar working together can produce very favourable results, and their affinity with each other gets enhanced this year. These two signs will make good business partners. Of the two, Rat will be luckier than Boar, and should take the lead in any endeavor they embark on together.

The EARTH SIGNS of **OX**, **DOG**, **DRAGON** and **SHEEP** all have good life force but bad spirit essence. This suggests that for these signs, they have decent inherent energy, but exposure to the wrong company could be harmful to their mindsets and their motivation levels. They are spiritually weaker than usual and need to carry the **"Om" Dakini Spirit Enhancing Amulet**. Those who are spiritual in nature can draw strength from their belief systems and find solace and comfort in their spiritual practice.

The **SHEEP** meanwhile is also in direct clash with the TAI SUI of the year, and hence the priority for this sign should be to take all steps to appease the God of the Year. The Sheep needs the **Tai Sui Amulet**, and its celestial guardian animal this year should be the **Dragon Pi Yao**. The

Tai Sui Amulet

Sheep can lean on its special friend the Horse, who enjoys superlative luck in 2021. The Sheep working or hanging out with a Horse in the coming year will benefit tremendously from its astrological soulmate. But all four Earth signs are in direct or indirect conflict with the Year God and should thus ALL carry the **Tai Sui Amulet** and have his plaque in the home.

WEALTH LUCK IN 2021

Wealth luck this coming year is weak. It will be difficult to make quick money. Wealth that gets created will come from hard work rather than speculative gains. The year continues to see much disruption to the way business is done, making things difficult for those in sunset industries. Individuals who can spot new opportunities can profit, but increasingly, the free flow of information will reduce the time window for monopolies in new industries. It will be creativity and originality, together with consistent hard work that will allow individuals and businesses to generate income in 2021.

As machines take over more and more jobs, those who do not do something and stubbornly hang on to an old way of life could quickly find themselves being made redundant. The year will not be an easy one for wealth creation, and macro level events continue to depress the immediate outlook.

Certain animal signs will have element luck in their favour when it comes to wealth luck this year; even so, the advice is to weigh all decisions carefully before making them. This is a year when one can take risks, but do not put all your eggs in one basket. Make sure any risks taken are calculated ones backed by understanding and research.

WEALTH ENHANCER: All individuals benefit from inviting in wealth enhancers, particularly the **Asset Wealth Bull** which boosts money and income luck, but also protects against your assets losing value. Those invested in the stock market would benefit greatly from the presence of this bull in the home. It has been designed to look like the stock market bull on Wall Street and carries the meaning "May the market bull for you"; it also features auspicious symbols of good fortune, a red saddle to represent prosperity in 2021, and it is shown presiding over a pile of coins and ingots, signifying its control and dominance over cash. With this bull, you will always have enough money, and even those who sustain losses will quickly make it back.

Asset Wealth Bull

GETTING YOUR TIMING RIGHT: It benefits the Horse greatly to carry the **"Black Tortoise" Constellation Lucky Charms**. Featuring the 7 Sky Animals from the Tortoise Constellation of the Lunar Mansions, these generate all the positive attributes of the Tortoise – support, endurance, stable wealth, longevity and good health – important in a year when the Horse has so much potential but with only moderate element luck indications. All you need this year to achieve your heart's desires is the correct motivation and staying power. When you have the Lunar Constellations on your side, it helps ensure you make all the right moves at the right time, so you do not get discouraged or distracted from your ultimate goals.

LOVE LUCK IN 2021
SINGLES CAN FIND LOVE IN 2021

For singles, this is a promising year for romance. The *Peach Blossom Star* has settled into the East, a WOOD sector, which gives it strength. The East is also the palace of the Rabbit, which is associated with the Moon and Moon Goddess who presides over fortunes related to love and romance. She bestows wishes to do with relationships, aids in matchmaking soulmates, and improves relations between married couples.

In 2021, the East becomes the place of the "Moon Rabbit" and enhancing this sector manifests love and romance for those looking for true love in their lives. Those wishing to settle down and get married, or searching for their soulmate or one true love, displaying the **Rabbit in the Moon** in the East will manifest this kind of luck for you.

MARRIED COUPLES BEWARE!!!

While there will be plenty of love and romance in 2021, it will not always be the kind that brings happiness. The year's chart also features the *Flower of Romance Star*. Unfortunately, it is the "external" version of this star – making all marriages vulnerable as there will be too much temptation from outside. Innocent flirtations can get out of hand, after-work drinks with colleagues or out-of-town business conferences can lead to inappropriate entanglements, spouses with the seven-year itch could be tempted to act on it. This is a year when those who are married should pay more attention to their other halves.

The *External Star of Romance* often affect those who have grown to take their marriage for granted. As long as you realise it, you can start taking measures to make things right. But what if an affair has already started?

CURE: We advise that when this troublesome star is present, married couples should make an effort to display symbols of marital stability and happiness in the home. All married couples should have the **Marriage Happiness Ducks** in the home, in the SW, East or center. Each can also carry the **Enhancing Relationships Amulet** to protect against third parties elbowing their way in and "crowding" the marriage.

Displaying the **"Rabbit in the Moon" Love Enhancer** in the home is also an excellent protective measure against stars that affect marital peace and happiness. In 2021, all couples can safeguard their marriage by displaying the Moon Rabbit with the full moon in

the East part of their home. For those who suspect their spouse is already cheating, you can call on the help of **Kurukulle**, the powerful Goddess of Love. Invoking her presence in your life imbues you with her talent for enchantment, giving you your power back when it comes to your spouse and your marriage. You can display her **Banner of Love** or carry the **Red Tara Home Protection Amulet** – this powerful talisman designed with her image and all her implements of love will repair damage already done to your marriage, while

Kurukulle's
Banner of Love

strengthening the bond between you and your spouse. Kurukulle's powers of magnetism will also make it difficult for others to adversely affect your marriage.

We also advise chanting her mantra daily:
OM KURUKULLE HRIH SOHA (21 times or 108 times)

STUDY LUCK IN 2021

To enhance study luck in 2021, students should call on the help of **Manjushri**, the Buddha of Wisdom. Manjushri with his wisdom sword slices through all ignorance in the mind, enhancing one's wisdom and knowledge. Invoking his help benefits not just students and those studying for exams, but also anyone needing to make important decisions and life choices. He clears the mind to make way for effective and efficient accumulation of knowledge – so that "your knowledge is vast, and your understanding complete". This year we have designed a **Manjushri Home Amulet** for scholars and students to place on their study desk. Manjushri's seed syllable is "DHIH" and chanting this repeatedly in one breath until you run out of breath is the best way to invoke his presence.

You can also chant Manjushri's wisdom mantra:
OM AH RAPA CHA NA DHIH

Make it a habit to chant his mantra either 21 times or 108 times (1 mala) before you sleep each night, or when you can find some quiet time during the day. We suggest you get yourself a **Manjushri Wisdom Mala** which you reserve specially for this purpose – chanting only Manjushri's Wisdom Mantra. This sharpens the mala's power and effectiveness when it comes to study luck, as the energies you direct into the mala as you chant becomes concentrated, making it more and more potent the more you use it.

HEALTH LUCK IN 2021

The Illness Star has flown into the North, the sector of the Rat. This affects all those born in Rat years, but also those whose main doors or bedrooms are located in the North of the home, or those who spend a lot of time in the North sector. Those afflicted with sickness or health problems should have the **Healing Deer** in the North.

Health risks continue to look like a threat going into 2021 so we have designed several potent health and protective talismans to keep everyone safe.

Our **mantra ring** this year features Medicine Buddha's mantra on the outside and Vairocana's mantra on the inside. Medicine Buddha comes to the aid of anyone who is sick and who calls to him for help. Vairocana is the Buddha that protects against contagious diseases. COVID-19 has been a life-altering phenomenon for the whole world throughout the last year, and as we move into 2021, it does not look like things will revert quite back to normal. We need to continue to practise vigilance following new guidelines as they get discovered to keep safe. Mask up, keep your social distance and get used to a new way of living.

The science of feng shui meanwhile always advocates protection before enhancement, so we strongly advise everyone irrespective of their animal signs to always wear or carry health and protective amulets. It can literally save your life!

 The **Medicine Buddha-Vairocana Mantra Ring** is excellent to help keep you safe during these strange times and troubled times.

This year we also strongly recommend the **Health Talisman with Tortoise and Snake**. The Tortoise and Snake are two spiritual creatures associated with longevity, known for their potent powers to heal. The tortoise provides stability both in physical and mental health, while the Snake represents control over the nagas, spirits that can cause ill health and sickness when they are left to their own mischievous devices.

All signs whose element luck tables indicate a poor health category should also place these health cures near to them or carry as portable amulets.

Element Luck of the Horse in 2021
Chapter 2

- Wood Horse – 7 & 67 years
- Water Horse – 19 & 79 years
- Metal Horse – 31 & 91 years
- Earth Horse – 43 years
- Fire Horse – 55 years

ELEMENT LUCK OF
THE HORSE IN 2021

The Horse's element luck in 2021 appears lacklustre. Nevertheless it is an improvement from last year when two of your most important categories of life force and spirit essence were negative. This year, these two categories have improved to a neutral reading. Your self-confidence returns and you begin to believe in yourself again. But because you are not particularly helped by your element luck, you will need to generate your own enthusiasm and get your own ball rolling.

To achieve success this year requires a great deal of effort, but because your other indications are excellent in terms of flying stars and the 24 Mountains, BIG success is exceedingly possible.

This is a year when you can meet your big break, when opportunities that come your way are quite exceptional. Making the most of these opportunities may be a little harder, but with the right conviction and mindset, a lot can be achieved by the Horse sign this year.

ELEMENT LUCK OF

	WATER HORSE 79/19 years	WOOD HORSE 67/7 years	FIRE HORSE 55 years
Life Force	neutral ox	neutral ox	neutral ox
Health	very good oo	excellent ooo	very bad xx
Wealth	excellent ooo	very bad xx	very good oo
Success	neutral ox	neutral ox	neutral ox
Spirit Essence	neutral ox	neutral ox	neutral ox

THE HORSE IN 2021

EARTH HORSE 43 years	METAL HORSE 91/31 years	2021 Element
neutral ox	neutral ox	Earth
neutral ox	good o	Earth
neutral ox	bad x	Metal
neutral ox	neutral ox	Water
neutral ox	neutral ox	Fire

The Horse needs to enhance ALL categories of element luck this year. You have to work at strengthening your inner and outer energy levels, and this means fighting the tendency to feel blasé about everything. Each day you need to get out of bed with a goal. Set yourself clear and definable objectives, ones that are easily measurable, because the Horse is the kind of sign that needs to see results. Results are what motivates you to keep going. You are a pragmatic sign, impetuous and impatient, and often, you don't have the staying power because you don't see the point.

This year, you need to work harder to see the wood for the trees, and to break down big goals into little ones. Horses do not like to work blind – you may be a work animal, but you are spontaneous and impulsive, unlike the Ox who intuitively compartmentalises bigger goals into distinctive steps. The Horse runs here and there, and often reacts to situations rather than making definitive plans.

If you can bridle all your enthusiasm and make a cohesive plan for yourself, you can draw on your inherent passion to achieve something truly noteworthy.

Some of the world's biggest and brightest names are Horse-born. Celebrity Horses include the likes of Nelson Mandela, John Travolta, Leonard Bernstein, Barbra Streisand, Condoleezza Rice, Jennifer

Lawrence, Sean Connery. All Horse-born individuals are built for fame and fortune, and shine bright and brilliantly on stage when put in the spotlight. But these last few years will not have been easy for the Horse-born, with affliction after affliction.

2021 is a year when you begin to emerge from the woods into the clearing, when your direction and sense of purpose returns. But you may still be weighed down by events of the recent past, which return to worry you in the form of lacklustre self-confidence and a lack of belief in yourself.

So the most important thing for the Horse this year is to rebuild that confidence. Strip away all that is fearful in you – what is it that you fear most? When you start to address your fears directly, you find they are small and not worth stressing about. But until you about turn to address them, they will linger like a dark shadow in your subconscious.

If the Horse can shed its hangups, 2021 offers the biggest and brightest year yet, when fame and fortune is yours for the taking. Remember, you have not one but TWO *Big Auspicious stars* blessing you from the 24 Mountains, and you are backed by the *Golden Deity Star*, affording you valuable assistance from the heavens.

For the Horse, the world is quite literally at your feet if you open your arms and accept all that you are worthy of. This will involve resilience and hard work, but your main obstacles will be mental ones. You have everything you need to do well – the skills, charisma, aptitude, passion. You just need to overcome your own self-doubt.

What the Horse needs is to have the **Victorious Windhorse Carrying a Jewel** to raise your success luck – this is the most potent symbol of success, especially since you are of the Horse sign. All Horse people should have the symbol of the

Victorious Windhorse

Windhorse close by, in front of you on your workdesk if possible, and carried as an amulet, or in your wallet in the form of a gold card. Make the Windhorse your personal talisman. This will boost your success luck will bring you all you can have and deserve this year.

2021 is a hugely promising year for the Horse. You have so many excellent indications. All you need to do is to strengthen your element luck and raise your lung ta to achieve all you are capable of. Think big, dream big, act big!

There is no spirit quite like the spirit of the Horse. You are passionate, fiery, headstrong, unpredictable – all the qualities that give you a distinct advantage over other signs, whether to achieve personal success, change the world for the better, or to make new friends.

You are the great adventurer of the Chinese Zodiac!

While the last two years may have been complicated due to setbacks of various kinds, this year, the sunshine returns. You feel unshackled from your tack, able to run free again. But some of you may be under your version of the *Stockholm Syndrome*. You may have gotten so used to your humdrum life, you've forgetten the joys of adventure, exploration and discovery.

Work this year at returning to who you truly are. Look back on the best years of your life and unearth the qualities that brought you those years. 2021 can be better than anything that came before!

The Horse needs the **Life Force Amulet** and **"Om" Dakini Spirit Enhancing Amulet** to boost these aspects of your luck. Your uninspired element luck will be the only thing holding you back, so work at overcoming this by improving your own inner and outer luck. Stay confident, generate your own passion, and work at sticking to your chosen path once you are on it.

This year, success for the Horse depends on the level of your passion and enthusiasm. If you have lost it, make extra effort to find it. When you engage your inner fire, the world is your oyster, truly! You have TWO Big Auspicious flanking you - don't waste these this year!

WEALTH LUCK
FOR THE DIFFERENT HORSES

Wealth luck differs for the different element Horses, but especially benefits the **79-year-old Water Horse** and the **19-year-old Water Horse** in 2021. These two Horses enjoy excellent element wealth luck, which suggests that financially you will be comfortable, and your wealth can grow. The **55-year-old Fire Horse** also has very good element wealth luck. To take full advantage, you should display the **Tree Bringing 3 Kinds of Wealth** in your living space; this will add growth energy to your wealth potential, boosting career and investment luck, and for some of you, even attract a windfall.

The **31-year-old Metal Horse** has a less robust indication in the wealth luck category. The advice for this Horse is to steer clear of risky investments.

For you, the best strategy is to maintain a sufficiently diversified portfolio and do not succumb to taking financial risks, no matter how irresistible, as luck is simply not with you when it comes to wealth in 2021.

The **67-year-old Wood Horse** has its wealth category at a VERY BAD level, so this is a warning to take serious steps to preserve your wealth. Avoid risky plays when it comes to money matters. This is not a year for frivolous expenditures. Unexpected and unavoidable expenses could crop up, disrupting your personal financial plan for the year. Be conservative, do not spend in excess, limit your exuberance when it comes to spending money. This Horse should carry the **"Hum" Dakini Wealth Protection Amulet**.

HEALTH OF THE HORSE

The only Horse with anything serious to worry about when it comes to health is the **55-year-old Fire Horse**. For this Horse, you should pay more attention to your health. Go for regular check-ups. If you don't feel well for any reason, get it looked at. Do not leave health concerns to a point when it is too late to do anything about it. While you may be active and feeling fit as a fiddle, do not take your health for granted.

This Horse should carry health amulets and have the **Medicine Buddha and the 7 Sugatas Gau** near you. Do not expose yourself to infectious viruses and diseases; post COVID19, you must absolutely not take any risks when it comes to your health. If there are quarantine recommendations in place, follow them! Don't be foolhardy and think you are invincible, because this year, health-wise, you are not.

An exciting year ahead awaits the Horse, but this is one when you must strengthen both your inner and outer resolve if you are to benefit from all the opportunities that are bound to come your way this year.

WOOD SNAKE 7 year old	
life force	neutral ox
health	excellent ooo
wealth	very bad xx
success	neutral ox
spirit essence	neutral ox

THE 7-YEAR-OLD WOOD HORSE

The Horse child is a boisterous little thing, full of spark and spunk and a big bundle of energy! If you are a parent of a Horse child, you will either be busy running after your young charge or you'll get a minder to do it in your place. The Horse is an independent-minded spirit, even from the earliest ages. If left completely to their own devices, they could run amok and possibly be a danger to themselves and others. There is no malice whatsoever in the young Horse, but plenty of mischief, as there is so much latent energy just waiting to bubble over.

The young Horse needs big open spaces and will tend to be extremely outdoorsy. Think headstrong young colt or filly and you get the picture. If you can channel all that energy into some sort of competitive sport, Horses can sail to the very top. They are naturals when it comes to sports, especially anything requiring athletic prowess. Running off their steam relaxes the young Horse's mind and improves their concentration for when they have to sit still.

This year is a fair one for the young Horse. Element luck is mostly neutral, so neither great nor terrible. But at this young age, element luck does not mean so much. Health luck is excellent, so as long as you keep this young 7-year-old occupied and sufficiently stimulated, the year will be a wonderful one to grow up in.

The 7-year-old Horse benefits from having images of its own animal sign of the Horse. Of particular benefit is the **Victorious Windhorse**, which lifts its success luck, which has only a neutral element showing this year. The young Horse also benefits from the **Dragon Carp**, a popular symbol of educational success for young children still developing life skills and acquiring knowledge.

Dragon Carp

WATER HORSE 19 year old	
life force	neutral ox
health	very good oo
wealth	excellent ooo
success	neutral ox
spirit essence	neutral ox

THE 19-YEAR-OLD WATER HORSE

The 19-year-old Water Horse can look forward to a terrific year! You have excellent wealth luck and very good health luck indications. All other categories are neutral, but these will tend to be pulled up by the encouraging wealth and health categories. You have little to worry about and should focus on gaining a good education, winning scholastic accolades and acquiring skills that equip you for the future. Make the most of this time of your life when you aren't yet burdened by the responsibilities of the adult world.

Do not try to grow up too quickly – there is still much to learn. Money will not be a worry for you. Even those of you who may not come from affluent backgrounds will find a way to get by. If you have the talent to study, and have the smarts but not the funds, don't lose hope. Be proactive, study hard, look for scholarships – for the Horse this year, when there is a will there is a way. Because your element luck is neutral but your other indications so fabulous, it may turn out to be a case of "all or nothing". *Winner takes all*. If you want to be among the winners, you have to put in superhuman effort, but think of it this way – the potential is there. You can be what you believe, and you achieve if your heart is in it all the way.

This young Water Horse has youthful determination on its side. Of all the Horses, you are the most amiable, going with wherever the flow takes you. You adapt well to every situation. This year, if you apply shrewdness to your decisions, you can well make life-changing decisions that set you up just the way you need for much greater success later on. You are at a turning point in your life, with the #1 Star backing you, indicating the germination of a really exciting new future. This is a time in your life when everything is possible. All you need is to match your opportunities with enthusiasm.

For the young Horse in 2021, hard work pays off like never before. Returns are out of proportion with the effort put in, making it more worthwhile than ever to try your very hardest this year!

This Horse benefits from the **6 Birds Big Auspicious Enhancer**. This harnesses the power of the Big Auspicious, helping you realize all your most fervent desires and wishes. You should also invoke the great **Buddha of Wisdom, Manjushri**. Carrying **Manjushri's "Dhih" Scholastic Amulet** will help guide you in making all the best decisions for your future.

METAL HORSE 31 year old	
life force	neutral ox
health	good o
wealth	bad x
success	neutral ox
spirit essence	neutral ox

THE 31-YEAR-OLD METAL HORSE

The 31-year-old Metal Horse has very neutral element luck this year, but wealth luck is lacking. Your wealth element luck has a negative showing, indicating you must not take risks when it comes to financial decisions. Not the best of years for the young entrepreneur Horse. Sales and profits are lackluster, but do not let this cause you to lose heart. It only means this is a year for planning and preparation. You are sitting on the #1 star which heralds new beginnings. This indicates the planting of new seeds, but seeds take time to grow.

This is a year when you can start new things, dream up new ideas, change direction in life if you so wish.

The Metal Horse is headstrong, restless and always raring to go. For you, your biggest problem is trying to play the waiting game. Rather than holding your fire till the time is right, you want to be constantly on the move. If you are in business for yourself, it would suit the young Metal Horse to have a more pragmatic partner to rein in your impetuous tendencies.

For your sign, the Snake and Sheep make good business partners this year – these two signs bring you the *Big Auspicious*. In addition, the Snake is your Fire element buddy, and the Sheep your soulmate and secret friend. Either of these signs will be extremely good for you this year.

The Metal Horse benefits from **Wealth Amulets** to boost your income and money luck. The **Asset Wealth Bull** will ensure your wealth can accumulate, ensuring you don't need to spend everything you earn, while the **Ox Finding Hidden Wealth** will allow you to tap opportunities you would otherwise not find in this year hidden gold. The **Camel** will avert danger of any cash flow problems. For those climbing the career ladder, having a **Gui Ren Amulet** on your desk will manifest a mentor figure in your life and bring you the help you need to progress in a professional capacity.

For the Horse, people born in years of the Snake and Sheep make great business partners this year.

EARTH HORSE 43 year old	
life force	neutral ox
health	neutral ox
wealth	neutral ox
success	neutral ox
spirit essence	neutral ox

THE 43-YEAR-OLD EARTH HORSE

The Earth Horse's element luck is neutral for all its categories of luck. This indicates that you have to generate your own enthusiasm for whatever it is you want to pursue. There is a sorrowful lack of external stimulus to get you going, so you have to generate all of your own excitement. Of the five kinds of Horses, you are the most grounded and down-to-earth. This makes you more stable and level-headed, but also less decisive. You are unlikely to take off on a whim unlike some of your Horse siblings, but you are also the most dependable.

The Earth Horse is the most domesticated variety of Horse, preferring the comforts of a warm barn than roaming the wilderness of the wild west like your mustang cousins. You are sociable and get along with many different circles in your life. You are as happy sipping champagne with dukes and queens as you are swigging beer in the local pubs. You are the ultimate politician, but your trouble will be finding a cause close to your heart. You are easily swayed to the opinion of others, which sometimes renders you indecisive about a lot of things.

When you have nothing to ignite your fire, it faces the danger of simply burning out.

This year, because the rest of your luck looks so promising, it would be a shame to let all that good fortune wind simply blow past you. There is plenty to achieve and to sink your teeth into, you just have to look harder and more closely to find it.

At work, make yourself more useful. Don't just turn up, cycle through the day then go home. Tap into your personal strengths and put them to good use. You have the diplomat's touch and when you work it, are able to fortify your position in any group you cultivate. To get ahead in your career, take a step back and start to spot where you may be most useful. Get to know your boss better, hang out with your peers after work, make friends with your colleagues.

For this Horse, you excel when you have the support of your herd, so go build your herd! You won't do this with force; rather, you win support with your subtle influence and indefatigable charm. But make it a point to get out there, mix, socialize, get busy. This is what will bring you back to life and to allow you to capture what 2021 has to offer.

This Horse needs the **6 Birds Big Auspicious Enhancer**. You also benefit from carrying the **8 Auspicious Objects Ru Yi** which will win you authority over those who become your supporters or followers. You have natural leadership qualities if you step up and harness them. When identifying objectives, do not let money be the deciding factor. There is little obvious wealth luck in your chart this year. But you have the ability to build something significant, something that will last and that can become a true legacy in the future.

FIRE HORSE 55 year old	
life force	neutral ox
health	very bad xx
wealth	very good oo
success	neutral ox
spirit essence	neutral ox

THE 55-YEAR-OLD FIRE HORSE

The 55-year-old Fire Horse enjoys very good wealth luck but very bad health luck. For you, this will be a year of balancing your enthusiasm with your well-being. You have much worth galloping after, but you must watch you do not burn out. Of all the Horses, you are the most flamboyant and most outwardly confident. You make an excellent politician and public figure. Wielding authority over others comes naturally to you. You are the life and soul of any party, and this year, you have the ability to convert the contacts you make into useful resources.

Lean on your naturally social tendencies; go out, make friends and widen your circles. You never know when you need to call on someone. This is a year when everything can be turned into an opportunity for you. Financially, you are in a strong position. You can invest with confidence because prosperity luck is on your side. In business, new initiatives driven by you are blessed by the hand of the divine. You have the luck of the heavens. You may want to boost this by carrying the **Dragon Heavenly Seal Amulet** and displaying the **Celestial Water Dragon** in the center of your home.

2021 is a year when you can convert your many bright ideas into reality. You work most efficiently when in charge, so engineer your life in a way where you take charge. Others are happy for you to take the lead if you seize the initiative.

This is a year when your lie-low period ends and your star begins to shine extremely bright again. The good thing about this Horse is that you will not allow temporary setbacks throw you too far off-course. You know when to stay under the radar, but when you reappear, you emerge stronger, recuperated and ready to face any new challenges thrust at you.

This is the year for the Horse to excel and to take center stage, and of all the Horses, the Fire Horse is best prepared for this this year.

The Fire Horse benefits from **Kuan Kung on Horseback**. Kuan Kung is the God of Wealth and War said to be the guardian saint of police and politicians, and also business leaders. He attracts prosperity luck and harnesses the power you need to get others on your side, and to keep them on your side. You also benefit from the **Life Force Amulet** and the **"Om" Dakini Spirit Essence Enhancing Amulet**. This Horse has a lot to look forward to this year.

WOOD HORSE 67 year old	
life force	neutral ox
health	excellent ooo
wealth	very bad xx
success	neutral ox
spirit essence	neutral ox

THE 67-YEAR-OLD WOOD HORSE

The Wood Horse is the friendliest and most amiable of the Horses. You get along with everyone, and this is what makes you so popular. You have plenty of friends and you make a skillful conversationalist. In 2021, your wealth luck continues to be woefully uninspiring, suggesting that this is still not the year to take financial risks or hope to make big money. If you shift your aspirations to ones that are less monetary and more spiritual in nature, you will be happier and feel more fulfilled.

Your health category however is excellent, indicating you have plenty of energy and impetus to pursue your passions. Just be careful when it comes to anything to do with money.

This Horse should refrain from gambling of any kind. Avoid speculating on the stock market. Do not risk your money. Chase your ideas by all means but do not throw money at it unless you are willing to lose it. A year when cash flow may become tight, not necessarily because you are making less but because you are spending more. Expenses could creep up without your noticing, and when credit card bills come at the end of the month, you could be in for a shock. Limit your spending. You do not have to give up your creature comforts, but you may have to hold back on your most extravagant tendencies.

The Wood Horse is a little bit of a show-off and sometimes you spend not for your own enjoyment but to keep up with the joneses. Shift your mindset and you will find it possible, even easy, to trim the monthly expense bill.

Spend this year pursuing a new skill or hobby. In regular times, travel and seeing new parts of the world would be a good suggestion, as would anything that expands your horizons, but if travel options are limited in the aftermath of the COVID19 pandemic, you can find new ways to push the envelope. Digital learning, online hangouts, courses for bosses.

This Horse should boost wealth luck with a collection of **Wealth Cabinets**. This will ensure your wealth can continue to grow and ensure you have enough should you reach a time when you want to retire or spend on a rainy day. You should also carry the **Good Fortune Lock Amulet** to protect against losing money or the **Pi Yao Wealth Amulet** to attract new sources of wealth into your life.

WATER HORSE 79 year old	
life force	neutral ox
health	very good oo
wealth	excellent ooo
success	neutral ox
spirit essence	neutral ox

THE 79-YEAR-OLD WATER HORSE

A very happy year awaits this Horse. You have excellent wealth luck and robust health luck, the two things required to ensure someone of your age has very little to worry about. This is a year to sit back and enjoy the fruits of your labour. Because wealth luck is good, this is an opportune time to spot new investment opportunities. But do back causes that you feel something for. Don't look purely for monetary gains. You will find that money alone will not be motivation enough. There is much to be said about psychic income and at your age, this is what will move you and mean something to you.

This is a year when you will enjoy spending more time with the family, your children and your grandkids.

Indulge them, get close to them, find things you have in common. Do not get offended by any generational gap you may feel. If you modify your conversation to their interests, not only will you find it easier to get close to them, you will find them breathing new life into your own being!

This Water Horse benefits from the **White Tara Gau Amulet**. White Tara is the Goddess of Longevity and brings a long life filled with good health, happiness and good fortune. She rids you of aches and pains and lethargy, and reinvigorates both body and soul. You also benefit from carrying the **Black Tortoise Lunar Mansion Talisman** which brings you good health and longevity luck.

Black Tortoise
Lunar Mansion
Talisman

Four Pillars Chart
2021
Chapter 3

FOUR PILLARS CHART 2021

An important indicator of the potential of any year is the Four Pillars chart of the year. This reveals the impact of the five elements of the year. When all five elements are present, it indicates a balance, a preferred situation. In feng shui, we are always striving for balance, and when something is out of balance, we always endeavor to bring things back into balance by introducing the missing element. This year, the chart

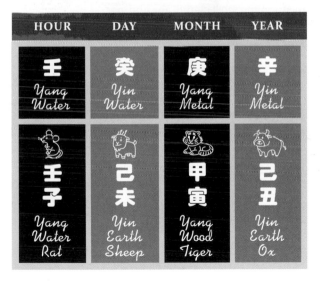

HOUR	DAY	MONTH	YEAR
壬 *Yang Water*	癸 *Yin Water*	庚 *Yang Metal*	辛 *Yin Metal*
壬子 *Yang Water Rat*	己未 *Yin Earth Sheep*	甲寅 *Yang Wood Tiger*	己丑 *Yin Earth Ox*

This year's Four Pillars chart lacks Fire, the element that signifies wealth luck.

is obviously missing Fire, the element that indicates WEALTH LUCK, so the year lacks opportunities to make money.

However, the eight characters in the Four Pillars – made up of 4 heavenly stems and 4 earthly branches – are not the only elements present. The interaction of these elements, depending on where and how they are positioned within the chart, generates a set of hidden elements as well as special stars. We use this chapter to analyse each part of this year's Four Pillars chart, and mention the most significant findings.

2021's Paht Chee chart indicates a strong self-element of Water, which boosts competitive energies and puts everyone on edge. Friends become foes when the stakes are raised, so this is a year to constantly watch one's back. The year's chart is unbalanced; it is missing the vital element of FIRE, which represents wealth and financial success. It is thus a year when it will be difficult to make much headway in the creation of new wealth. Profits may take a long time to get realized and there are few speculative gains to be made.

Prosperity comes with hard work rather than with a stroke of luck. This is definitely not a year to strike it rich via the lottery.

Here is a closer look at the most important indications this year:

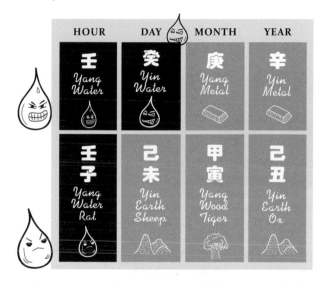

There appears to be way too much Water in this year's chart.

A YEAR OF STRONG WATER
indicating a competitive year

First, the self-element of the year is Strong Water. It is a year when rivalry becomes enhanced and when politics can get unscrupulous. Watch your back and reserve your trust for your very innermost circle. Indeed, even your inner circle could let you down if the circumstances dictate. Betrayals happen of their own accord, sometimes without the guilty party's conscious intention. Learn to forgive and move on but protect yourself by being more careful and by putting safeguards in place. Remove temptation where you can and stay close to all you are working with.

PROTECTION: Those in business are advised to carry the **Kuan Kung on Horseback Anti-Betrayal Amulet**. This will protect you against the betrayal of others and being let down by people whom you trust. It keeps you prepared for whatever the winds and waters bring your way.

In any competitive endeavour, it could well feel like a fight to the death. Diplomatic compromises will be difficult to achieve, and different factions and interest groups find it harder to reach win-win scenarios. But it is nevertheless important to try. Sometimes being the bigger person will help; but recognize when you have to fight and when you don't. Indeed, do not mistakenly think you are in fact being the magnanimous one when you are being taken for a fool. It is a year when it is prudent to carry protection always. The **28 Hums Protection Amulet** is an excellent all-round amulet that will safeguard you from all kinds of harm.

SOLUTION: The excess of Water energy in the chart needs to be resolved. Use **WOOD energy** to weaken the excess Water. Having plenty of greenery and live plants in your living space will help re-balance the energies and will also bring vital growth energy to a year which lacks the presence of the *Lap Chun*, or "Spring".

This year, having plenty of plants and Wood energy in the home will help soak up the excess Water in the year's chart.

BALANCE OF YIN & YANG

Second, there are two Yang pillars and two Yin Pillars.
There is thus a good mix between energetic periods
and restive ones, with no dominance of work over
play, or vice versa. The Yang Month and Hour Pillars
bring great vitality, while the Yin Year and Day Pillars
bring balance. There should be more than enough
strength to propel positive chi forward and upward.
People in general are open to different viewpoints.
If negative energies can be kept under control and
sufficiently subdued, the year is then able to propel
forward, benefitting many.

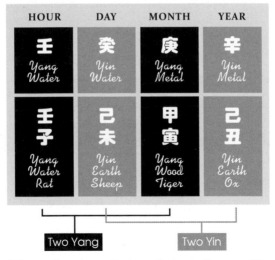

This year there is good balance between Yang and Yin
in the year's Four Pillars chart.

CLASH OF SHEEP WITH OX
indicating strong conflict energy

Third, there is a clash of SHEEP with OX in the Earth Branches. This clash between two Earth animals suggests that the clash will be between leaders. Earth is the element that represents leadership and rank, thus animosity will likely be between those who are in charge. But because those in power are especially strong this year, fighting can become ferocious, with the damage dealt far-reaching. There will be strong clashes between the leaders of nations.

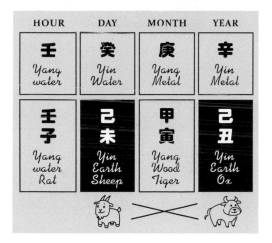

The clash between Ox and Sheep brings many problems to the year, especially between those who are in charge and everyone else, who could end up as collateral damage.

Within family units, because the clash occurs in the Day Pillar, there is likely to be strong conflict between spouses.

SOLUTION: There may be more marital problems in 2021 with the Sheep in the Self-Spouse pillar clashing with the Year pillar. In the family unit, this coupled with the presence of the *External Flower of Romance* star brings all kinds of problems to husband and wife. Every home this year should have the **"Rabbit in the Moon" Love Enhancer** and better still if both husband and wife carry the **Enhancing Relationships Amulet**. Recognize when an outsider is trying to make trouble in your marriage, and refrain from siding with a third party over your spouse, no matter how much your husband or wife may be annoying you. When you allow an outsider into the mix, this year, such troubles can escalate very quickly.

Enhancing
Relationships Amulet

SPECIAL LINK BETWEEN RAT & OX
bringing creativity and inventiveness

Fourth, there is however a very strong affinity between RAT and OX in the Earthly Branches of the Year and Hour Pillar. This is a heaven sent because it serves to repair some of the damage resulting from the Ox-Sheep clash. The Year Pillar of the Ox forms a soulmate pairing with the Hour Pillar of the Rat, which means there is a good beginning and a good ending to the year, what the Chinese refer to as having a head and tail, a suggestion that things that

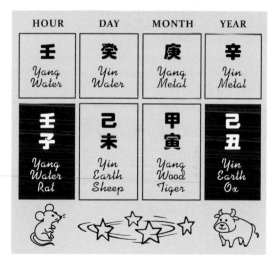

HOUR	DAY	MONTH	YEAR
壬	癸	庚	辛
Yang Water	Yin Water	Yang Metal	Yin Metal
壬 子	己 未	甲 寅	己 丑
Yang Water Rat	Yin Earth Sheep	Yang Wood Tiger	Yin Earth Ox

The Rat and Ox in this year's chart form a very special affinity, bringing relationship and completion luck.

get started have a good chance to reach satisfactory completion. The two signs of Rat and Ox are extremely harmonious together, generating the *House of Cleverness and Creativity*, with the Rat starting and the Ox completing. This endows the year with wonderful ingenuity and inventiveness.

> The presence of the Rat & Ox in the year's Four Pillars suggests a year when true friendship means something.

These two signs are also a secret-friend pair, indicating **good friendship luck** through the year. While there are indications of strong competition and rivalry, there is also much potential for firm friendships, and opportunities for friends to demonstrate their loyalties and allegiance. A year perhaps of finding out who one's true friends are.

ENHANCER: Get the **"Perfect Partnerships to Attract Big Wealth" Enhancer**. This enhancer featuring the Ox and Rat will boost all the positive indications of this combination. Display in a prominent area in the home; in the living room, or near the dining room where you spend a lot of time. The number "8" on the Ox activates for the missing wealth luck of the year.

NO PROSPERITY LUCK INDICATED
... but there is hidden wealth

Fifth, there is MISSING WEALTH. Fire which represents wealth is completely missing from the main chart. What this indicates is that it will be difficult to make money. New businesses will take time getting off the ground, sales will be slow, industries that are shrinking will continue to do so, while their replacements will take time to take flight. Profit margins get squeezed as information becomes more and more freely available, and technology continues to disrupt at breakneck pace. This year, if one wants to stay afloat, it is vitally important to keep up with the world that is so rapidly changing around us.

While there will be results and completions, it will nevertheless feel like an interim year, because we are at the beginning end of a new cycle, and not quite at the close of the current period. 2021 represents the second animal sign of the cycle after the new decade last year opened with the Rat, and we are heading towards the end of Period 8, and the beginning of Period 9, but we are not quite there yet.

There is a lack of obvious wealth in 2021, but those who look harder can find gold. This year, there is HIDDEN WEALTH brought by the sign of the TIGER.

While WEALTH luck may be lacking, there is however HIDDEN WEALTH brought by the TIGER. This will bring some respite, and keep us tided over, but it is wealth that comes in its own time rather than overnight. What this means is that 2021 is a year when we can lay the foundations for future wealth, but we must not get our hopes up for immediate results.

That the hidden wealth star is brought by the Tiger bodes well for friends of the Tiger – the Dog and especially the Horse.

The Dog enjoys one *Small Auspicious Star* from the 24 mountains chart, while the Horse enjoys not one but *TWO Big Auspicious Stars*, together with a *Golden Deity Star*. These two astrological allies of the big cat are lucky in this respect in terms of money-making prospects, although all signs can boost wealth luck with suitable activators and enhancers.

THE COLOUR FOR WEALTH: The wearing of the most auspicious colour of the spectrum RED will bring significant added benefits in 2021. Red is the colour which represents ultimate YANG, which serves to boost the year's vitality, but will do double duty in enhancing the missing Wealth element of the year. Red in 2021 stands for WEALTH, so wearing this colour as part of your wardrobe or accessories will give

For Wealth

you a boost of good fortune. You should also carry the **"Increase Your Wealth Luck" Gold Talisman Card** featuring the God of Wealth Tsai Shen Yeh seated on a Tiger. This will attract wealth of the kind that keeps increasing and will help you tap the hidden wealth luck of the year.

You can also display the **Bejewelled God of Wealth sitting on a Tiger** in figurine form in the home.

Bejewelled God
of Wealth sitting
on a Tiger

Before the New Year arrives, make sure you get our specially created **Red Wealth Wallet** featuring the Wealth Ox. It is auspicious each year to change to a new wallet and especially lucky to take some money from your old wallet and transfer it over to your new wallet. Doing so for this year will ensure you take some of the energy of last year, and carry it over into the following year. In 2021 you definitely want to do this, as the previous Year of the Rat carried two *Lap Chuns*, or two "Springs" while this year has none.

Keep the lights in your home brightly turned on throughout the year, especially in the WEST sector, which plays host to the Prosperity Star #8.

POWERFUL SPIRITUAL ENHANCER: For Wealth Luck that is potent and long-lasting, an excellent ritual to incorporate into your life is the **White Dzambala Ritual**. Invite in **White Dzambala and the Four Dakinis** who pull in

wealth from the four directions. Display in a respectful place in the home and recite White Dzambala's mantra as regularly as you can.

White Dzambala's Mantra:
Om Padma Krodha Arya Dzambala
Hridaya Hum Phat

When you gaze upon him and chant his mantra regularly, he manifests great riches in your life and attracts incredible opportunities that can bring wealth of a big meaningful and lasting kind.

INVITE IN THE ROOSTER: The Rooster brings the #8 Wealth Star in 2021, so it is extremely auspicious to have many images of Roosters in the home this year. The Rooster is also the symbol that ensures politicking is kept to a minimum, protecting against harmful gossip and slander. The Rooster is also wonderful for protecting the marriage, preventing any troublesome third party from trying to come between husband and wife.

Rooster with Crown

There are many benefits to displaying the Rooster this year; indeed, it may be a good time to start collecting Roosters, made of different colours and in different materials if you wish. You can also display Rooster Art in the home, which is most auspicious. Display in the West part of the home.

Our new **Rooster with Crown** this year has been embellished with powerful symbols of protection and good fortune, to ensure the negative energies of the year cannot harm you. It features the "Anti Evil-Eye" to protect against jealousy, the Double Dorje for wisdom in decision making and the powerful "Hum" seed syllable for strong protection. Its powerful feathers sweep away all harmful energies and its crown symbolizes holding dominion over the year.

LUCKY SPECIAL STARS OF 2021

Sixth, there are two potentially VERY AUSPICIOUS stars in the year's Four Pillars chart. These are seriously good stars noted for being strong and very explicit in their beneficial influence. These stars have the capability of bringing incredible good fortune to those who know how to activate them correctly, while making sure the positive aspects of their influences materialize.

These stars impact different animal signs differently and in varying degrees, but are nevertheless very beneficial for all signs. Note that you will need to wear or carry the relevant activators to ensure that you make the most of the positive influence of these stars.

THE STAR OF PROSPECTS
brings many new opportunities

This star brought by the Earthly Branch of Rat in the Hour Pillar with the self-element of Water indicates many new opportunities in the coming year. This favourable star conjures up a very special energy that rewards determination and staying power, resonating

HOUR	DAY	MONTH	YEAR
壬	癸	庚	辛
Yang Water	Yin Water	Yang Metal	Yin Metal
壬子	己未	甲寅	己丑
Yang Water Rat	Yin Earth Sheep	Yang Wood Tiger	Yin Earth Ox

The Star of Prospects brings many new opportunities in the coming year.

with the Ox sign of the year, a reminder that those who retain their passion for success will benefit from its presence. This star suggests there is nothing that cannot be achieved for those prepared to work hard. The more ambitious one is, the further one can go this year.

STAR OF PROSPECTS: To activate this star in your favour, keep an **image of an Ox** near you. We suggest the **Bejewelled Asset Bull** to magnify wealth luck and to ensure the hard work you put in meets with proportionate success. This bull has been designed with an auspicious saddle in red, the colour that signifies wealth in 2021, wearing a harness of coins and stepping on a pile of wealth and ingots, symbolizing the accumulation of assets.

This beautiful enhancer will allow you to accumulate everything you work for and ensure you do not spend everything you earn. It will also increase the opportunities that come your way.

THE STAR OF POWERFUL MENTORS
brings Benefactor Luck

The Star of Powerful Mentors which was also in last year's chart makes another appearance in 2021. This star is brought by the OX in the Year Pillar and the Heavenly Stem of YANG METAL in the Month Pillar. This star is especially beneficial for the younger generation, who have the auspicious luck of influential people turning up in their lives to help them, giving them meaningful advice and powerful support.

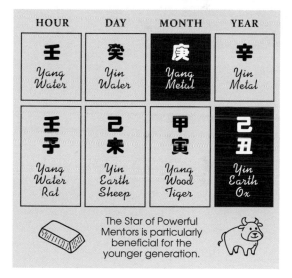

HOUR	DAY	MONTH	YEAR
壬	癸	庚	辛
Yang Water	Yin Water	Yang Metal	Yin Metal
壬子	己未	甲寅	己丑
Yang Water Rat	Yin Earth Sheep	Yang Wood Tiger	Yin Earth Ox

The Star of Powerful Mentors is particularly beneficial for the younger generation.

For students hungry for success, mentors will open doors to scholarship, and teachers will provide fabulous inspiration and motivation. Opportunities abound and there will be unseen hands supporting you. Those just starting out in your careers can find a mentor figure to guide you and to show you the ropes. An influential boss could fast-track your promotion up the ranks.

ACTIVATE THE STAR OF POWERFUL MENTORS: Bring this star to life by displaying **Kuan Kung** in the home. You can also display near to you work or study desk. Another powerful activator for this star is the **Nobleman Qui Ren Talisman**. The

benefits of this special star are immense, so it is worth activating. It brings help from the heavens, manifesting someone in your life with the wish and means to help you, and ensures those with this kind of power stay firmly on your side.

AFFLICTIVE STARS OF 2021

There are two unlucky stars brought by the Four Pillars chart of the year. These, when not attended to with relevant cures, can wreak a lot of havoc and create a lot of misfortune, but their ill influence can be avoided if you take special note and address them.

THE AGGRESSIVE SWORD STAR
is a Double-Edged Sword

The Aggressive Sword Star formed by the Yin Water in the Heavenly Stem of the Day Pillar and the Earthly Branch of Ox in the Year Pillar suggests a year of

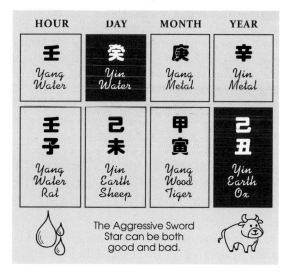

HOUR	DAY	MONTH	YEAR
壬	癸	庚	辛
Yang Water	Yin Water	Yang Metal	Yin Metal
壬 子	己 未	甲 寅	己 丑
Yang Water Rat	Yin Earth Sheep	Yang Wood Tiger	Yin Earth Ox

The Aggressive Sword Star can be both good and bad.

intense aggression. It indicates the strengthening of the underdog's chi, so it points to a rise of revolutionary fervour, people revolting against authority. Strikes continue, spawning groups around the globe to walk similar paths. Protests advocating for greater equality, non-discrimination, fighting against police brutality and other social injustices continue to pick up steam. There will be anger, passion, rioting and violence.

At its pinnacle, the presence of this star suggests the emergence of powerful leaders on opposing sides, or of highly influential opposition to established leaders. It suggests the rise of a people who seize power by fair means or foul. The name of this star is *Yang Ren*, which describes *"yang essence sharp blade that inflicts damage"*. This is a star with great potential for either very good or very bad influences to materialize during the year, although generally, the influence tends to be more negative than positive. There is risk of revolution and of the toppling of unpopular leaders in power.

> The Aggressive Sword Star brings potential for violence & bloodshed. This star must be strongly subdued.

In this year's chart, the *Star of Aggressive Sword* is created by the strong YIN WATER of the DAY pillar, with the presence of the OX in the YEAR pillar. Here, note that the WATER element is strong in the chart, making the presence of the Aggressive Sword much more negative. It indicates that those emerging as leaders for the underdog in 2021 will end up being heavy-handed and quick-tempered. They may be charismatic but they will also be strong-willed, conceited, arrogant, overbearing and self-centered - all nasty traits that spell the potential for bloodshed and violence wherever they emerge. There is real danger of this this year!

CURE: To shield against the harmful effects of the Aggressive Sword Star, the best remedy is a powerful spiritual Stupa. The **Kumbum Stupa** is especially beneficial as it contains one hundred holy images, invoking the protection of all the world's Wisdom Protectors. This Stupa will ensure that all family members living within the home stay protected against aggression or violence of any kind. It is also a good idea to wear or carry the **28 Hums Protection Wheel Amulet** at all times.

Kumbum Stupa

THE FLOWER OF ROMANCE STAR (EXTERNAL) *makes marriages vulnerable*

This star is sometimes confused with the *Peach Blossom Star* because it addresses the destiny of love; but while both influence love and romance, they are very different in their effects. When the Flower of Romance is present, it suggests love blossoms easily, but it is not the kind of love that leads to marriage and family. It indicates instead the possibility of extramarital affairs, bringing stress and unhappiness to married couples. There is also a difference between *internal* and *external romance*, and in this year of the Ox, it is unfortunately the latter that prevails. So the year

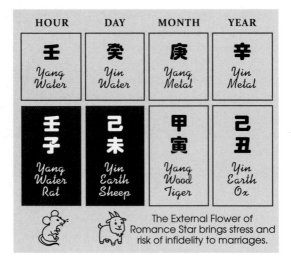

HOUR	DAY	MONTH	YEAR
壬	癸	庚	辛
Yang Water	Yin Water	Yang Metal	Yin Metal
壬子	己未	甲寅	己丑
Yang Water Rat	Yin Earth Sheep	Yang Wood Tiger	Yin Earth Ox

The External Flower of Romance Star brings stress and risk of infidelity to marriages.

is likely to see increased occurrences of infidelity and break-ups of marriages.

Marriages are vulnerable to the External Flower of Romance this year.

The SHEEP in the Day Pillar and RAT of the Hour Pillar indicate the presence of the *External Romance Star*, making all marriages vulnerable to straying by husband OR wife. Things are made worse as the Sheep clashes with the ruling animal of the year, the Ox. This causes misunderstandings between couples, and danger of an outsider fanning the flames from the side.

FIXING THE EXTERNAL STAR OF ROMANCE: To prevent this affliction from doing real harm to your marriage, carry the **Enhancing Relationships Amulet**, especially if you suspect your spouse already has eyes for someone outside your marriage. Or if you are constantly fighting with each other, or forced into a situation when you have to spend large amounts of time apart (e.g. if one of you commutes to a different country for work, or travel a lot for work). It is also a good idea to display a pair of **Marriage Happiness Ducks** in the SW of the home, or if you suspect something has already started, place an **Amethyst Geode** tied with red string under the foot of the bed of the straying partner.

You can also invite in the **image of an Ox and Horse** to counter the affliction. This subdues the possibility of infidelity causing problems for you. The OX/HORSE presence will create a special "cross" with the SHEEP/RAT affliction.

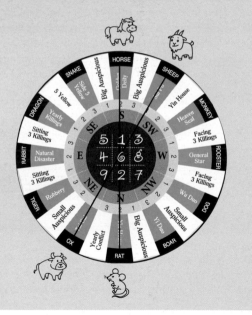

Flying Stars of 2021
Chapter 4

FLYING STAR CHART OF 2021
Heavenly Star *rules the year*

The Flying Star chart on first glance is a big improvement on last year's chart. The Loss Star #7 of 2020 makes way for the *Heaven Star* #6 in this Year of the Ox 2021. The Heaven Star becomes the dominant star of this year. This white star is associated with many good things, attracting the celestial luck of the heavens and providing the unseen hand of opportunity and guidance from above. Everyone stands to benefit from this star, especially if the center of the home where the star is located is kept well-energized and active throughout the year.

In 2021, it benefits to keep the center of the home very active! Have friends over & use this space well.

Rearrange your furniture so you naturally gravitate to the center of your home. The more you include this space in daily usage, the better the luck of the whole family for this coming year.

2021's chart suits homes with open plan layouts arranged around the center part of the home. This is where the luck of auspicious heaven energy congregates this year, and keeping this part of the home lively and vibrant with lots of music, chatter and activity will serve to "activate" this star, bringing it to life!

Work at repositioning your furniture and seating if you have to. This year it is extremely auspicious for all members of the household to spend plenty of time in the center sector, and when you have guests, entertain them in this part of the home. If your home has a piano, place it in the center so every time someone sits down to play it, the sector gets energized.

If your home is not an open-concept one, keep the doors to the center room in the home ajar as much as possible.

You want the energy that emanates from the center to seep into all other areas of the home. The more you energize this part of your house, and the more you suppress the bad luck sectors, the better the luck of the whole household for the year.

ENHANCE THE CENTER GRID
with the Celestial Water Dragon

This year, every household benefits from the presence of the **Celestial Water Dragon**. Place this celestial creature in the center of your home and of your office. The celestial Dragon is the ultimate symbol of good fortune and its deep blue colour and cloud imagery suggest its heavenly origins. This Dragon is auspicious wherever he is displayed, but this year he especially benefits the center part of the home, which houses the Heaven Star #6.

The Celestial Water Dragon is the best enhancer for the #6 Heaven Star which occupies the central sector in 2021.

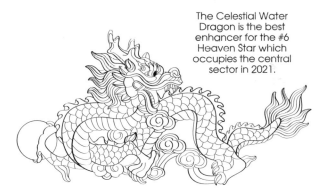

Placing the Celestial Water Dragon here will attract plenty of new and lucrative opportunities into your life, as well as the patrons, mentors and contacts you need to support you in whatever path you choose to take. Individuals and organizations who are in a position to help you and to open doors for you, will somehow find their way into your life. The presence of the celestial Dragon always attracts abundance and success, and this year, inviting in this Dragon brings a very special kind of good fortune indeed.

Invoking the power of
THE EIGHT IMMORTALS

Another excellent energizer for the center is the **8 Celestial Immortals Plaque**. The 8 Immortals bring eight kinds of good fortune and protects against harm. In Chinese mythology, they are a revered group of legendary beings each with a unique talent or ability.

Place the 8 Immortals Plaque in the center
of the home in 2021.

These eight saints have been depicted in Chinese art since time immemorial as they are believed to bestow wealth, longevity and spiritual awakening on all who glance upon them.

Depicted as a group, they bring a balanced basket of good fortune and protection for the whole family. They hail from the 8 different compass directions and are usually shown with their unique symbols representing the luck each brings.

Zhang Guo Lao, protector of the North, **brings the luck of good descendants**. His symbol is the bamboo flute and his element is Water. He enjoys drinking wine and is famous for making his own which had curative and healing powers. He is said to be able to drink poison without harm and offers protection against the dark arts. He is often shown with his companion, the mule.

Chao Guo Jiu, protector of the Northeast, **brings the luck of control**. He is excellent for those in positions of authority who have to motivate and retain the support of those they command. His element is Earth and his symbol are the castanets. According to legend, he went to great lengths to avoid casualties of war, protecting the innocent from harm during battle. He is skilled in the magical arts and possesses great wisdom and charisma to lead with great authority.

Lee Dong Bin, protector of the West, **brings protection against evil**. His element is Metal and his implement is the Magic Sword. He is famed for being a great scholar and poet, and for his exceptional intelligence. While he had certain character flaws – he was a serial womanizer - he was known for his dedication to helping others elevate their spiritual growth.

He Xian Gu, protector of the Southwest, **bestows family and marriage luck**. Her element is Earth and her symbol is the Lotus Blossom. The only lady among the 8, she has also grown to become a symbol of woman power. She is often accompanied by a mythical bird said to reign over all birds, bringing new opportunities from near and far. She helps stabilize married couples, protecting the sacred sanctity of marriage and bestowing a happy family life. She protects against troublemakers who threaten to break up happy families. For those who are single, she is said to attract marriage opportunities and suitable suitors.

Han Xiang Zi, protector of the Southeast, **brings healing energies** to those who are sick, but more particularly, he helps heal those with a broken heart. His element is Wood and his symbol is the flute. His legendary past involves the tragic love story where he fell in love with the daughter of the Dragon King, who did not grant the couple his blessings. Theirs was a star-crossed romance without a happy ending, but the bamboo flute he wields was said to be a gift from his beloved. Playing on his flute healed him emotionally, and from there on he vowed to help others the same way.

Lan Chai He, protector of the Northwest, **brings scholastic and creative luck**. His element is Metal and his symbol the flower basket. He is often shown with his swan, symbolic of his lyrical gifts. He is said to have become immortal when the Monkey King bestowed 500 years of magic upon him. His companion is the Monkey. As well as his flair for the arts, he is said to possess a sharp intelligence and wit.

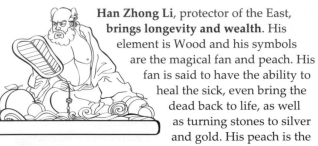

Han Zhong Li, protector of the East, **brings longevity and wealth**. His element is Wood and his symbols are the magical fan and peach. His fan is said to have the ability to heal the sick, even bring the dead back to life, as well as turning stones to silver and gold. His peach is the fruit of immortality which grants a long life filled with happiness.

Tie Guai Lee, protector of the South, **brings wisdom and healing**. His element is Fire and his symbol is the Bottle Gourd. He is often depicted as an unkempt old man with disheveled hair, taking on the appearance of a beggar. His chosen role is to care for those who are sick, poor or in need.

Enhance for Future Prosperity
in the Northeast

The animal sign of the year, the Ox plays host to the *Future Prosperity Star* #9. This star signifies imminent wealth just about to ripen, and the closer we get to Period 9, which starts Feb 4th 2024, the shorter the waiting time for what is considered "future wealth". The #9 is also a magnifying star, which gains power as we head into Period 9. The Ox sign this year thus gets energized with the presence of this star in its sector. The NE is also the place of the Tiger, who features as always in the year's Paht Chee in the month pillar.

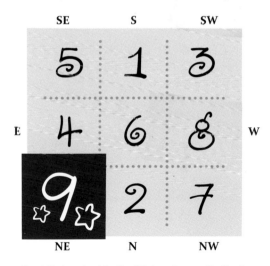

The NE plays host to the "Future Prosperity Star".

The powerful Fire star #9 brings vitality to all who come under its influence, and its presence in the ruling animal sector bodes well for the coming year. This star benefits homes that face NE, and individuals whose bedrooms or office rooms are located NE, as well as those born under the signs of Ox and Tiger.

The #9 in the NE suggests that the central #6 heavenly star gets strengthened. This is a lucky star for most of the year, except for months when monthly flying stars here are unfavourable – i.e. March, May, July, August and December 2021. When unfavourable monthly stars visit, ensure you have the relevant cures in place and keep this sector less active during these times.

ENHANCERS FOR THE NORTHEAST

The NE benefits from the **9 Golden Dragons Plaque** featuring nine celestial Dragons that bestow power and generates the capacity to pursue all one's grandest ambitions conviction and courage.

Having nine Dragons in the NE allows you to stay focused on long-term goals without getting distracted,

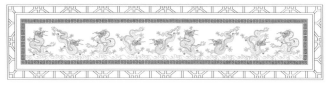

Display the 9 Golden Dragons Plaque in the NE.

or discouraged by short-term difficulties. They protect you against those who wish to see you fail, and shields you from the effects of less ambitious relatives or acquaintances who do not have your vision.

Displaying this plaque in the NE of your home or office ensures you have the support of not one but *nine* Dragons, the number that symbolizes completion and abundance. The number 9 is a magical number as it is a number that always reduces back to itself when multiplied. It also strengthens the #9 star, which is getting stronger as we move rapidly towards a fast-approaching Period of 9.

BUILD YOUR WEALTH: You should also activate the NE with a collection of **Wealth Cabinets**. These wealth cabinets symbolize an accumulation of asset wealth, meaning that the money you make accrues into ever-larger amounts that can last into the many generations. Energizing the NE helps you to make enough money so you do not have to spend everything you earn. It allows you to grow wealthy enough to carve out a secure, comfortable and worry-free future for yourself and your loved ones.

Activate for Love & Romance
in the EAST

The Peach Blossom Star #4 settles into in the East sector this year. This star gets greatly enhanced in 2021 as the East is the place of the Rabbit, the creature associated with the Moon, and with the Goddess of the Moon who governs all fortunes to do with love, romance and relationships. Legend has it that when you catch the attention of the Moon Goddess, she aids you in all matters related to the heart, improving relations between lovers and even matchmaking those who are destined to be together.

The East plays host to the Peach Blossom Star, which brings romance.

For those who are single, activating this sector with the **Rabbit in the Moon** awakens the powers of **Moon Goddess**, alerting her to all wishes to do with affairs of the heart. Enhancing this sector promotes the success of relationships, attracts marriage opportunities, smooths interactions between spouses, and imbues stale marriages with a newfound passion and vigour.

> The EAST becomes the place of the MOON RABBIT in 2021, harnessing the power of the Lunar Mansions to bring great love and romance into the lives of those who activate this luck.

This is the sector to enhance if love is what you are looking for! This year we have designed the **Rabbit in the Moon**, the earthly messenger of this lunar goddess. Placing this activator in the East will help singles meet their soulmates and forever partners, while helping those who are already married to keep their spouses.  Remember that this year's Paht Chee generates the unfavourable *External Flower of Romance Star*, which can cause problems within already existing relationships, resulting in unwanted love triangles and other outside disturbances to a love relationship. Invoking the blessings of the **Rabbit in the Moon** ensures that only the positive aspects of love materialize. It will also protect against unpleasantness associated with matters of the heart. They say there is nothing sweeter than love, but they also say that nothing breaks like a heart – remember the song by Mark Ronson and Miley Cyrus? Heartache and heartbreak can be far more painful than physical pain; the #4 in the East brings the Moon Rabbit to life and provides a solution for those looking for happiness in love.

ATTRACTING MARRIAGE OPPORTUNITIES

For those looking for a soul mate, someone you can settle down with and make a future with, or if you are already dating but your partner seems a long way off from proposing marriage, you can speed things along with the help of your **Peach Blossom Animal**. Our new Peach Blossom animals the **Rat**, **Rabbit**, **Horse** and **Rooster** come with trees of fortune enhanced with potent symbols of love and marriage.

The **Peach Blossom Rabbit** brings love and marriage opportunities to the **Horse**, **Tiger** and **Dog**. If you are looking for love that leads to marriage, or you would like your current partner to propose, display a **Peach Blossom Rabbit** in the EAST in 2021.

Peach Blossom Rabbit

For students,
activate the Scholastic Star in the EAST

For young people and anyone pursuing their studies, engaged in research or in search of new knowledge, they can activate the scholastic star of the year which flies to the East in 2021. The #4 is also the star number that brings study and exam luck; when properly activated, it has the power to help you achieve success in anything related to scholastic accolades. Enhancing this star improves clarity of mind, allowing you to absorb new knowledge and to process it with much greater efficiency. Anything requiring cognitive

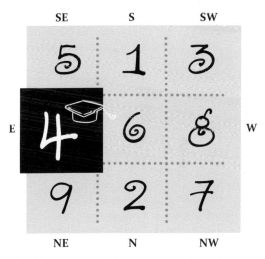

The #4 star in the East is also the Star of Scholarship

reasoning and abilities gets enhanced when you harness the energies of this star number.

The #4 Scholastic Star also boosts creativity and original thinking, allowing you to better come up with unique and innovative new ideas. This star gets strengthened this year, as it is a Wood star flying into a Wood sector.

ENHANCE THE SCHOLASTIC STAR: The best way to activate the #4 for scholastic luck is to carry **Manjushri's Gau**. Manjushri is the Buddha of Wisdom, and when you call on his help, he slices through your ignorance so only wisdom remains. His flaming sword removes all that is obscured in your mind, allowing you to think with a clear head so you can map out effective solutions to everything you are pursuing.

For students taking exams, having Manjushri's support enables them to recall everything they have revised and studied, and to write excellent answers in their exam. Manjushri boosts everything to do with wisdom and intelligence, and helps one to make wise choices. He ensures one constantly sees the big picture, while also filling in the details. For school-going children, they can clip **Manjushri's Amulet** onto their schoolbag. The specially-designed **Scholastic Amulet with Manjushri's mantra** sums up all of his wisdom and blessings, providing an endless stream of support, reinforcement and inspiration.

FOR EXAM LUCK:

For students taking important exams and hoping to do well, there is no better enhancer than the **Dragon Carp**. The carp that jumps over the Dragon Gate and successfully transforms into a Dragon is the best symbol of success for anyone aspiring to scholastic success. It promotes the luck of the scholarship and helps students not just pass exams but excel in them. The Dragon Carp also generates a strong sense of self-motivation, ensuring one does not fall into bad company or get side-tracked into unproductive tasks. This is the best enhancer for children or teenagers looking to perform well in important exams, to win awards, to gain scholarships and grants and to gain admission into colleges of their choice.

The academic path of today is filled with potholes and pitfalls, far more than in the old days, as everything has become so much more competitive. More and more young people are fighting for fewer places at the top universities and colleges; at school, children are faced with competition from classmates with Tiger parents in the sidelines egging them on. For a young mind, it can all become too much, and with all the expectations heaped on young shoulders these days, sometimes all it takes is one bad test or one bad result to cause a child to throw in the towel and just give up.

As parents, we need to imbue in our children not just the impetus to keep striving for the top, but help them understand there will be bumps and disappointments along the way. It is not necessary to perform every single day of the year, to come out top in every single test; what is important is to peak when it counts. The **Dragon Carp** stabilizes one's mind, helping a child along the academic path and to navigate all that comes his or her way with a strong and mature mind, resulting in success when it truly matters.

Transform Five Yellow Misfortune Star
in the Southeast

The bogus star, the Five Yellow, makes its way into the Southeast this year. The good news is that because the Southeast is a Wood Sector, it mitigates the extent of damage of this dangerous Earth star, as Wood destroys Earth in the cycle of elements. When the Five Yellow flies into a Wood sector, misfortune can be turned into opportunity. This is why we have designed this year's **Five Element Pagoda with a Tree of Life**. This alters the effects of the *wu wang*, suppressing the darker side of this star while

SE	S	SW
5	1	3
4 (E)	6	8 (W)
9	2	7
NE	N	NW

The 5 Yellow afflicts the SE in 2021 but with the correct cure, this Five Yellow has the potential to bring great good luck!

harnessing its benevolent powers. This star affects those living in homes that face SE, those with bedrooms or work rooms in the SE, and those born in years of the Dragon and Snake.

If your house has more than one level, make sure you have a **Five Element Pagoda with Tree of Life** on every floor. Keep the SE of the home free from too much activity and noise, and avoid renovations in this part of the home in 2021. Whatever you do, DO NOT renovate the SE of the home this year.

Victory Star brings winning luck
to the South

The White Star #1 associated with victory and winning luck makes its way to the South. This star allows you to triumph in any situation and to attain success over any competition you may face. In 2021, this star benefits those whose bedrooms are located South, and all those living in homes that face South. Anyone who spends a lot of time in this part of their home can also tap into the good luck this star brings by keeping it well energized with the correct activators. The livelier you keep this part of the home, the better!

The Victory Star this year is made more potent as it is supported by not one but **TWO Big Auspicious Stars** from the 24 Mountains, as well as the **Golden Deity**

The South sector enjoys the Victory Star in 2021.

Star, echoing the benefits of the ruling star of the year, the #6 Heaven Star. All this serves to increase the power and effectiveness of this star, so it is really worthwhile to actively enhance this star. Because the South is the sector governing the reputation of the household, the #1 here also improves one's standing and repute in various circles – work, social, etc.

ACTIVATE THE VICTORY STAR:
The best enhancer for the Victory Star is the **Victorious Windhorse Carrying a Jewel**. The Windhorse is the very essence of success luck, known as the magical steed of the folk hero King Gesar, who when riding his Windhorse could never be defeated. His horse with flaming red coat has become synonymous with success and victory, and his image is what is needed whenever one needs to boost one's chances against others in any kind of competitive situation. In 2021, we recommend for everyone the Victorious Windhorse to place in the South. This sector is also the home sector of the Horse, an auspicious creature that emanates pure Fire energy. Displaying images and figurines of horses in the South is thus very appropriate and auspicious indeed.

Activate the #1 Star in the South with the Victorious Windhorse

BOOST POWER AND AUTHORITY:
For those in positions of leadership and management, the best way to enhance your effectiveness as a leader is with the help of the **Ru Yi**. The Ru Yi is the royal scepter of power, which bestows "the right to rule". In ancient China, anyone in any kind of power would never be seen without a Ru Yi at his side. You can place your Ru Yi in front of you on your work desk, or carry in your bag.

The **Crimson Red Ru Yi with Bats** brings the luck of **success and abundance**. Any boss, head or leader can use the help of this Ru Yi to ensure things between all in their group stay harmonious, joyful and productive at all times. It attracts the luck of abundance and success, so whatever is pursued turns out fruitful and effective. It helps you to ensure all your final goals are reached in the most harmonious way.

Anyone in any kind of leadership position needs a Ru Yi.

The **Deep Blue Ru Yi with 8 Auspicious Symbols** brings the luck of **wealth**. This Ru Yi includes the Victory Banner for winning luck, the Double Fish for abundance, the Parasol for protection, the Conch for good news, the Wheel for sustainability, the Mystic Knot for longevity, the Vase for completion and the Lotus for good intentions.

These symbols of good fortune are the magical implements of the Eight Immortals, and act as vessels of their power. Carrying images of their magical symbols on a Ru Yi imbues you with a complete collection of the different kinds of luck you need to reach your full potential as a leader.

The **Yellow Ru Yi with Celestial Dragon** brings the luck of **power and position**. Those operating in political environments or in politics need this Ru Yi! It bestows charisma and magnetism, and endows strength to make your position one that is stable and secure. It ensures you do not get plotted against and overthrown. It protects against betrayal and treachery and gives you power over those on the outside as well as on the inside.

The SOUTH is the place to activate if success, victory, fame and reputation is what you seek.

Suppress the Quarrelsome Star
in the Southwest

The Quarrelsome Star #3 flies to the Southwest, bringing hostile energy and complications associated with arguments, misunderstandings and court cases. The #3 star can also cause serious aggravations that lead to violence and tragedy. This affliction affects anyone with a bedroom in the SW, those whose main doors face SW, and those born in years of the Sheep and Monkey. It also affects the Matriarch of the household. The #3 star is especially strong this year,

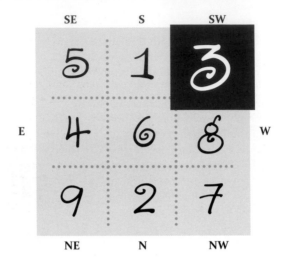

Beware the #3 quarrelsome star in the SW this year.

as the intrinsic Wood energy of the star dominates the Earth energy of the SW. The effects of this star are made worse as the SW also plays host to the **Yin House** from the 24 Mountains. All this suggests that this affliction MUST be taken seriously.

Anything that suggests Fire is an effective cure, so keeping the lights turned on brightly in this sector will help combat the negative energies of this star. **The colour red** is also suitable, so red curtains, rugs and cushion covers here will help very much indeed.

CURES FOR THE QUARRELSOME STAR:
For 2021, the best remedy for the Quarrelsome Star in the SW is the **Nine Phoenix Plaque** in red and gold. These celestial birds in red and gold - which represent the elements of Fire and Metal - work to subdue this troublesome Wood Star. The Fire energy engulfs the Wood of the #3, while the Metal energy of the gold effectively subdues it.

The Nine Phoenix Plaque is an excellent cure against the #3 Quarrelsome Star.

We also recommend placing **red carpets** in this sector, or in the SW portion of any room you spend a lot of time in. Another effective cure for the #3 are the **Red Peace and Harmony Apples**. In Chinese, the word for peaceful is *Ping*, which sounds like the word for apple – *Ping Kor*. This year's Peace Apples comes embossed with the English word "Peace" and the Chinese rhyming couplet carrying the meaning "If your intentions are good and your heart is pure, the world will be peaceful."

Place this pair of apples in the SW to ensure all members of the household stay supportive of one another, and to prevent clashes and conflict from arising. Also an excellent cure for use within the office to maintain a productive and supportive environment between colleagues and workmates.

Enhance Prosperity Star 8
in the West

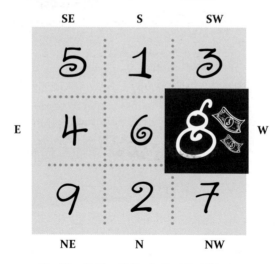

The Wealth Star #8 flies to the West this year.

The very lucky Wealth Star #8 makes its way to the West, the sector of the Rooster. This star is also known as the *Current Prosperity Star*, as we are currently in the Period of 8. The West is the sector that represents children and descendants, suggesting that the wealth this sector brings will last into the long term, reaching future generations and for many generations to come. It points to a successful accumulation of assets over time if properly energized.

In 2021, the West can be considered one of the luckiest areas of the home, because it enjoys this auspicious #8 star. The strong energy of the current period emanating from this sector benefits all homes whose main entrances face West, and all bedrooms and offices located in the West benefit from this luck. The West is also the place of the youngest daughter, so the wealth this sector brings benefits the young girls of the house.

> WEALTH luck takes root in the WEST sector this year, so this is the area of the home you should enhance for greater prosperity luck.

Remember that to activate the luck of this auspicious star #8, the West should be thoroughly imbued with yang energy - this means lots of activity, lots of noise and plenty of bright lights. When there is movement, sound, chatter and merry-making, the number 8 comes to life, bringing good fortune and big prosperity. In the constellations, 8 is a "man-made star" with two assistants – on the right and on the left - so that at its strongest moments, it brings wealth and great nobility.

When the 8 can turn dangerous...
Beware however. The number becomes negative when afflicted by structures in the environment that threaten its location. If the West sector of your home has too much Metal energy, or if there are harmful physical structures that cause poison arrows to direct threatening energy your way, that is when the number 8 can bring harm to young children especially young daughters of the household, causing illness to arise. If there are such structures external to your home, but towards the West, it is important to block the view

with curtains, or dissipate the killing energy with **facetted crystal balls**. These will disperse the worst of the killing breath before it has the chance to enter your home.

If the view from your window to the WEST is of a threatening looking building with sharp edges or poison arrows, keep the curtains in this area closed to block the offending view from spoiling your feng shui. Hang facetted crystal balls here.

ACTIVATE FOR WEALTH IN THE WEST

The best way to manifest wealth luck in 2021 is the make sure the West part of your home is well-energized with wealth symbols. Because this is the year of the Ox, this creature is especially lucky as it symbolizes harnessing the good fortune of the year. Because the West represents children and descendants, this prosperity luck benefits the whole family not just in the present but into the long term.

The image of the Ox has great power to attract abundant good fortune in 2021. Displaying images of the Ox in all sizes and permutations is so lucky this year! For the collectors among you, a good time to start "collecting" Ox images.

A fabulous wealth enhancer for this year is the **Asset Wealth Bull**. This Bull holds the symbolic and subliminal message "May the market bull for you"! With resplendent red saddle and surrounded by coins, ingots and symbols of prosperity, this bull energizes for wealth of the kind that can accumulate into expanded net worth, the kind that provides meaningful disposable income, providing a worry-free future.

Display the Asset Wealth Bull for wealth that grows and expands your net worth!

To tap the hidden wealth of the year, display the **Ox finding Hidden Wealth**. This Ox is depicting calmly and unobtrusively grazing in a field full of coins, sniffing out hidden wealth and opportunities. In a year with little obvious wealth but a lot of hidden wealth, this Ox generates the luck that allows you to tap the full potential of the year.

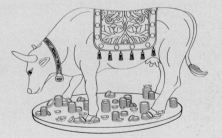

Invite in the "Ox Finding Hidden Wealth" to tap the full potential of the year.

Another great activator for this year's wealth star is the **Tree Bringing 3 Kinds of Wealth**.

Trees always depict growth energy, and when they look like money trees, they really do bring the luck of wealth into the home! Our tree this year has been designed to represent the manifestation of 3 different kinds of wealth - Asset Wealth, Income Wealth and Growth Wealth. Having all three kinds of wealth brings you not just enough to lead a comfortable life now, it gives you security and peace of mind and allows you to plan for the future. This year's wealth tree also features 12 lucky charms to signify abundance in all forms entering your life - the Double Fish, the Apple, the Treasure Chest, the Golden Ingot, the Wealth Vase, the Abacus, the I-Ching Coin, Gold bars, the 4-leafed clover the Maneki Neko Lucky Cat and the Pot of Gold.

This year's wealth tree represents not just prosperity luck but also the luck of asset accumulation. This symbolises your wealth growing and your networth expanding.

Beware Betrayal & Loss Star
in the Northwest

A dangerous aspect of this year's chart is the #7 Robbery Star in the NW. This brings loss and betrayal energies to the Patriarch, which not only means the patriarch of the family, but leaders, bosses, managers and anyone responsible for the welfare or livelihood of others. The presence of the #7 in the NW suggests that the Patriarch could get cheated, conned or betrayed. It brings the energy that suggests you should keep your friends close but your enemies closer.

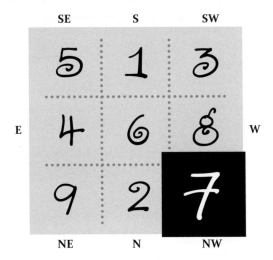

The NW, the sector of the Patriarch and Leader, gets afflicted by the #7 Loss and Betrayal Star in 2021.

In 2021, keep your friends close but your enemies closer!

Stay alert like a hawk, as treachery can strike at any moment. The energies of the year could corrupt even the most trustworthy of friends and the most loyal of employees. The #7 Robbery Star, like its namesake, describes a situation when you are cheated out of money; but it can also manifest as an actual robbery. We recommend all who stay out late, or who venture anywhere even remotely unsafe, to carry the **Nightspot Protection Amulet**. Because this star affects the NW, it harms the Father the most, but there can be knock-on adverse effects on the rest of the family, or the rest of a leader's charges.

CURE FOR #7 STAR: This year the best cure for the #7 star in the home is the **Anti-Burglary Plaque with Door Guardians**. These Door Gods with spear in the ready are depicted with the Anti-Burglary Amulets, with the Chinese proverb, "May your family be blessed with peace, safety and abundant joy, may your home be filled with everlasting happiness."

Display in the NW to ensure your home stays protected against unexpected and unwanted intruders, who may cause not just loss of property and possessions, but loss of peace of mind. These door guardians will help keep your family protected through the year.

BEWARE BETRAYAL:

This year, risk of betrayal is rife as the #7 star occupies the NW, the location of the leader. Betrayal means duplicity from those you trust, those you least suspect and therefore those you are most vulnerable to. While it feels nasty to get cheated by conmen and people you do not know, when betrayals come from those closest to you, the harm is emotional as well as physical. The loss is no longer merely monetary, it hits a nerve deep within that can be difficult to take and recover from. This year, because opportunity for this to happen gets increased, we suggest to remove temptation where you can, watch your back, and carry symbols to protect against this kind of bad luck. Carry the **Kuan Kung Anti-Betrayal Amulet**. This specially-designed talisman features the amulet that protects against being stabbed in the back, with the mantra that ensures the protection is effective.

Kuan Kung on horseback
Anti-Betrayal Amulet

PROTECT AGAINST BEING CHEATED:
For those engaging in high-risk deals carry the **Anti-Cheating Amulet** to ensure you do not get conned by unscrupulous people. An excellent amulet for business people and for anyone dealing with new acquaintances who maybe be untrustworthy.

PROTECTION AGAINST THE DARK ARTS:
Another form of harm can come from those who practice black magic. Especially in the East, such arts are more common than you think. Even if you do not subscribe or "believe" in this kind of power, it exists. Someone who projects negative thoughts against you, whether out of spite, jealousy or some other reason, does not even have to be skilled in these methods to send negative hexes and projectiles your way!

For example, if someone curses you on the street because they are angry at the way you drive, this can result in the same kind of misfortune effect as someone actively plotting or using black magic against you. The latter is of course more serious, but whenever one is weak in terms of spirit essence and element luck, they can succumb badly when someone forms negative thoughts and sends those thoughts their way.

The best protection against this kind of harm is the **28 Hums Protection Wheel**, which features the powerful **Heart Sutra** on the back. These sacred syllables together with this powerful sutra ensures that whatever projectiles are sent your way cannot reach you. A vital cure for anyone with enemies, who are engaged in high stakes deals, or anyone who may have offended someone intentionally or unintentionally.

28 Hums
Protection
Wheel

Suppress Illness Star
in the North

The #2 Illness Star flies to the North, and because North is of the Water element, it cannot do anything on its own to weaken the energies of the #2, an Earth star. The Illness Star is further strengthened as it is supported by the **Yin House Star** in North 2, the sector of the Rat. This boosts the potency of this star, making the North sector dangerous for those who are elderly, frail or prone to illness.

Big Auspicious

N

Yin House

RAT

Yearly Conflict

It is important for anyone whose bedroom is facing North, or whose home faces North to suppress the Illness Star with strong cures.

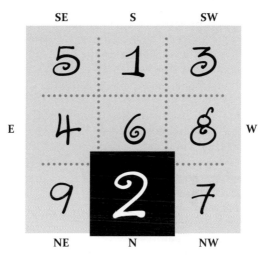

SE	S	SW
5	1	3
4	6	8
9	**2**	7
NE	N	NW

(E on left, W on right)

CURE FOR THE ILLNESS STAR:
In 2021, a good cure for the Illness Star is the
**Healing Deer Carrying Vase of Longevity
with Linzhi**. The deer is renowned
by the Chinese for their powerful
curative properties and is often
seen as the companion of the God of
Longevity, Sau Seng Kong. With the
world caught up in fears of epidemics
and pandemics where there seems no
escape with a proper cure a long time

Healing Deer

coming, the deer is an excellent shield against this kind of illness. Display in the North of the home this year. The Healing Deer is an excellent symbol of good health in the year 2021.

Another potent cure against the Illness Star #2 is the **Medicine Buddha & 7 Sugatas Gau**. Medicine Buddha always comes to the aid of those who are suffering when one calls for his help. His area of expertise is in the removal of poisons, disease and illness, and the **Medicine Buddha & 7 Sugatas Gau** features all 8 of his emanations, and his powerful mantras in whole. You can place in  the North of the home to stay under his protection constantly. Excellent for anyone who is ill or feeling unwell.

You can also chant his mantra daily:
TADYATHA OM BHEKHANDZYE BHEKHANDZYE MAHA BHEKHANDZYE (BHEKHANDZYE) RADZA SAMUGATE SOHA

For those suffering from a chronic ailment, we suggest that you get yourself a dedicated **Medicine Buddha Mala** to chant with. The more you chant his mantra over the mala, the more powerful the mala will become. Keep the mala with you always, and whenever you have spare time, bring it out and chant. You can also wear the mala as an accessory around your wrist or neck.

HEART MANTRA
OF ARYA VAIROCHANA

WOFS™

AGAINST COVID-19: To protect against the coronavirus specifically, the best cure is to invite in an image of the **Buddha Vairocana**, who brings blessings of good health but also provides strong protection against contagious diseases. Display his image as a figurine, and also carry his image in the form of a **Gold Talisman Card** which we have made available to help tide us through these challenging times.

AFFLICTIONS OF 2021
TAI SUI *in the NORTHEAST*

The TAI SUI or God of the Year always occupies the sector of the ruling animal sign of the year. This year, he occupies the palace of the Ox, Northeast 1. The Tai Sui is the celestial force that governs all that happens on Earth, and when one has his support and blessings, very little can go wrong, but when one offends him, his wrath knows no bounds.

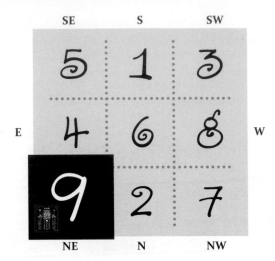

The Tai Sui resides in the NE this year, and it is important to keep him on your side. Place the Tai Sui Plaque 2021 here.

It is a matter of course and tradition for most Chinese who believe, to offer prayers to Tai Sui at the start of the year, humbly asking for his help and support for the coming year. In feng shui, the creature that is known to appease him is the celestial chimera the **Dragon Pi Xie**, so we always recommend to place this in the location of the Tai Sui.

The Dragon Pi Xie is said to appease the Tai Sui. Place in the NE in 2021.

PROTECTION: What is even more important is to place the **Tai Sui Plaque** with his image and invocation as a sign of respect. In 2021, place this in the NE1 sector. Animal signs especially affected by the Tai Sui this year are the Earth signs of Sheep, Dragon and Dog, while the Ox whose location he occupies should also be mindful of his presence there. For these 4 signs, we also recommend carrying the **Tai Sui Amulet** at all times throughout the year.

THREE KILLINGS in the EAST

This affliction is said to bring three types of misfortune – loss of wealth, loss of reputation and loss of a loved one. All three are devastating, and when not one but three forms of bad luck hit you at once, the loss can be difficult and extremely distressing. This is another affliction that is important to take note of and to cure.

Firstly, NEVER have your back to the Three Killings affliction, so in 2021, DO NOT SIT FACING WEST,

EVEN if WEST is your best direction! Do not sit with your back to the East, as the Three Killings is the kind of affliction that stabs you in the back, when you are least suspecting. It carries the characteristic of hitting you when you are most comfortable and least aware. When things are at their calmest, beware, because the storm is about to pound and crash down...

NEVER HAVE YOUR BACK TO THE EAST this year! Make sure you do not get stabbed by the dangerous 3 killings affliction!

CURE FOR THE THREE KILLINGS: Place the **3 Celestial Shields** to combat the Three Killings.

These shields act as effective armour sheltering you from the effects of this difficult affliction. All homes should display these shields in the EAST of the home in 2021. Anyone with something to lose, who operate where stakes are high, or who are going through years of low element luck are also recommended to carry the **3 Celestial Shields Amulet** when on the go. Use as a keychain or bag decoration.

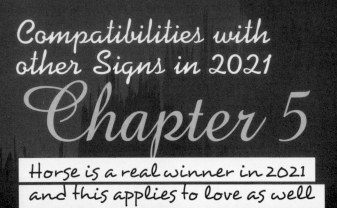

Compatibilities with other Signs in 2021

Chapter 5

Horse is a real winner in 2021 and this applies to love as well

The Horse enters a wonderful year feeling really on top of the world! Everything improves after a run of very mediocre past few years. In 2021, Horse's luck does a complete turnaround and if you embrace the good energies coming to you, the year holds out so much success and many victories; and if you're looking for love, the start of a wonderful new romance. A good year for thinking of marriage and settling down. Your other relationships also improve. When the Horse sign is confident and spirited, its mood rubs off on all it interacts with. Make the most of this year to make new friends, strengthen current relationships and most importantly, enjoy yourself!

Many different influences come into play each year to determine how one animal sign gets along with another. Chinese astrology has so many permutations that it is difficult to take note of everything, but examining some of the main variables can give useful insights to the general mood and compatibility between any two signs in any year. The annual energies of the year have a larger bearing on the effect on your relationships than you may be aware of, and understanding these effects allows you to be more effective in all your interactions.

When you find the keys to unlock what makes your connections tick, not only will this help with your happiness levels, it also improves your productivity and success potential.

Every animal sign under the Chinese Zodiac system has certain signs they are naturally drawn towards; certain signs make better spouses, others make more exciting lovers, others still work better when you remain platonic friends. Certain pairings thrive in a business relationship, as boss and employee, mentor and mentee; others work well as parent and child, siblings, sporting teammates or drinking buddies; while others still, have the potential to change your life in a big way.

There are also certain signs you need to stay alert to and be wary of. One's Zodiac Adversary is the animal sign born six years apart from you, the sign directly opposite you in the Zodiac wheel – but in certain years, your "natural enemy" can become a useful ally, while in others, you would be best advised to stay well clear of each other. Having knowledge of how the year's energies influence your relationships will give you an edge when it comes to how you relate to others in any given year.

In this section, we analyse the relationship between the Horse and the other signs of the Zodiac, looking in particular at the quality and nature of the relationships as determined by the influences of 2021.

1. Alliance of Allies

There are four affinity groupings that form natural allies in the horoscope. The three signs in each group have similar thought processes, aspirations and goals. Their attitudes are alike, and their support of each other is immediate and instinctive. If there is an alliance within a family unit amongst siblings, or between spouses and their child, the family is incredibly supportive, giving strength to each other. In good years, auspicious luck gets multiplied.

Astrological allies always get along. Any falling out is temporary. They trust each other and close ranks against external threats. Good astrological feng shui comes from carrying the image of your allies, especially when they are going through good years.

ALLY GROUPINGS	ANIMALS	CHARACTERISTICS
Competitors	Rat, Dragon, Monkey	Competent, Tough, Resolute
Intellectuals	Ox, Snake, Rooster	Generous, Focused, Resilient
Enthusiasts	Dog, Tiger, Horse	Aggressive, Rebellious, Coy
Diplomats	Boar, Sheep, Rabbit	Creative, Kind, Emotional

When all three signs in a particular year has good fortune, the alliance is strengthened. But in years when one sign stands out with superior luck, the others in its grouping can "lean" on that sign to lift itself up. The Horse belongs to the grouping of Enthusiasts in the Zodiac, comprising the Tiger, Horse and Dog.

This year, the strongest link in the Horse's alliance of allies is the Tiger, who has the most promising element luck in the group. For the Horse, friends born in the year of the Tiger become a very good influence on you, and brings you good fortune luck.

In 2021, the Horse can lean on the Tiger to gain strength. It favours the Horse to fraternize with friends born in the year of the Tiger. The excellent element luck of your ally the Tiger gives you a boost of confidence and a line to significant contacts and opportunities.

If you do not have close friends or alliances born in a Tiger year, you can simulate this luck with the image of the Tiger. Wearing Tiger amulets or displaying the Tiger in your living space brings you much good fortune luck this year. Because the Tiger is closely related to many wealth gods from the Chinese pantheon of deities, displaying Tigers accompanying these wealth deities brings not just relationship luck to the Horse but wealth luck as well.

The Horse benefits from the presence of the Tiger in 2021. This is your astrological ally enjoying superlative element luck this year, and keeping a Tiger close allows you to "borrow" some of this luck.

2. Zodiac Soulmates

Another natural ally for you is your Zodiac soulmate. In Chinese astrology, there are six pairs of signs that create six Zodiac Houses of yin and yang soulmates. Each pair creates powerful bonding on a cosmic level. Marriages or business unions between people belonging to the same Zodiac House are extremely auspicious. In a marriage, there is great love and

HOUSES OF PAIRED SOULMATES

ANIMALS	YIN/ YANG	ZODIAC HOUSE	TARGET UNLEASHED
Rat & Ox	YANG /YIN	*House of Creativity & Cleverness*	The Rat initiates The Ox completes
Tiger & Rabbit	YANG /YIN	*House of Growth & Development*	The Tiger uses strength The Rabbit uses negotiation
Dragon & Snake	YANG /YIN	*House of Magic & Spirituality*	The Dragon takes action The Snake creates magic
Horse & Sheep	YANG /YIN	*House of Passion & Sexuality*	The Horse embodies strength & courage The Sheep embodies seduction & allure
Monkey & Rooster	YANG /YIN	*House of Career & Commerce*	The Monkey creates good strategy The Rooster takes timely action
Dog & Boar	YANG /YIN	*House of Domesticity*	The Dog creates alliances The Boar benefits

devotion, and in a commercial partnership, it promises much wealth and success. Such a pairing is also good between professional colleagues or between siblings.

The strength of each pair is different, each having a defining strength with some making better commercial than marriage partners. How successful you are as a pair depends on how you bond. The table on the following page summarizes the key strength of each Zodiac house.

For the Horse, your Zodiac Soulmate is the Sheep. Together you form the *House of Passion & Sexuality*. Your relationship is characterized very much by passion and sexuality, so yours will be a highly-charged romantic affair, fuelled by your libidos. The Sheep gets carried away by the sexual overtures of the Horse, but being together also brings out passion for some joint project or emotional cause that gets you both going.

In this partnership, the Horse embodies the male energy while the Sheep embodies the female energy. So you bring out the deeper sides of one another. Together you create *nien yen*, what Feng Shui Masters describe as excellent marriage and family luck, the kind that brings many descendants. A marriage between Horse and Sheep will have sexuality as the central focus that binds them, but the cosmic energy created will add much to your combined luck.

3. Secret Friends

Another extremely powerful affinity arises when two secret friends come together. There are six pairs of secret friends in the Zodiac. Love, respect and goodwill flow freely between you. Once forged, your bond is extremely hard to break. Even when you yourselves want to break it, it will be hard for either party to walk away. This pair of signs will stick together through thick and thin.

For the Horse, your secret friend is the Sheep. This relationship is doubly special because the Sheep is not just your secret friend, but your soulmate as well.

Horse and Sheep will be successful transforming every moment into something romantic and magical. You enjoy a happy family life constantly filled with new and happy surprises. The two of you will enjoy a special

PAIRINGS OF SECRET FRIENDS

🐀	Rat	Ox	🐂
🐖	Boar	Tiger	🐅
🐕	Dog	Rabbit	🐇
🐉	Dragon	Rooster	🐓
🐍	Snake	Monkey	🐒
🐎	Horse	Sheep	🐐

bond that others will envy. This will be a very happy pairing that is especially helpful when one of you may be going through a hard time or when health issues cause one to lose energy or willpower to stick through a tough situation.

The secret friends pairing are like Zodiac best friends. Symbolically, the presence of your secret friend creates the chi of attracting good friends into your life.

4. Peach Blossom Links

Each alliance of allies has a special relationship with one of the four primary signs of Horse, Rat, Rooster and Rabbit in that these are the symbolic representations of love and romance for one alliance group of animal signs. These are referred to as Peach Blossom Animals, and the presence of their images in the homes of the matching alliance of allies brings peach blossom luck, which is associated with love and romance.

For the Horse, because the Rabbit is your Peach Blossom link, displaying images of rabbits in the home brings love and marriage luck. The Peach Blossom Rabbit is an excellent version, as this rabbit is symbolic of true love.

> The Horse belongs to the alliance of Tiger, Horse and Dog, which has the Rabbit as their Peach Blossom link.

The Horse benefits from placing images of the Rabbit with Peach Blossom in the East part of the house, or in the Horse direction of South. Another excellent image is the **Moon Rabbit**. This rabbit brings love and marriage luck to all animal signs, but especially to the Horse.

5. Seasonal Trinities

Another grouping of signs creates the seasonal trinity combinations that bring the luck of *seasonal abundance*. To many experts, this is regarded one of the more powerful combinations. When it exists within a family made up of either parent or both parents with one or more children, it indicates that as a family unit, their collective luck can transform all that is negative into positive outcomes. When annual indications of the year are not favourable, the existence of a seasonal

ANIMAL SIGNS	SEASON	ELEMEMT	DIRECTION
Dragon, Rabbit, Tiger	*Spring*	Wood	East
Snake, Horse, Sheep	*Summer*	Fire	South
Monkey, Rooster, Dog	*Autumn*	Metal	West
Ox, Rat, Boar	*Winter*	Water	North

Seasonal Trinities

combination of signs in any living abode can transform bad luck into better luck, especially during the season indicated by the combination. It is necessary for all three signs to live together or be in the same office working in close proximity for this powerful pattern to work. For greater impact, it is better if they are all using the direction associated with the relevant season.

The Horse belongs to the Summer Season, its direction is South, and its seasonal group comprises the Snake, Horse and Sheep.

6. Astrological Enemies

Your astrological enemy is the sign that directly confronts yours in the astrology wheel. For the Horse, your astrological enemy is the Rat. Note that your enemy does not necessarily harm you; it only means someone of this sign can never be of any real help to

PAIRINGS OF ASTROLOGICAL ENEMIES		
Rat	⟷	Horse
Boar	⟷	Snake
Dog	⟷	Dragon
Rabbit	⟷	Rooster
Tiger	⟷	Monkey
Ox	⟷	Sheep

you. There is a six year gap between natural enemies. A marriage between astrological enemies is not usually recommended. Marriage between a Horse and Rat is unlikely to bring lasting happiness unless other indications suggest otherwise. The Horse is advised to refrain from getting involved with anyone born in the year of the Rat, although on a year-by-year basis, this can sometimes be overcome by the annual energies.

As a business partnership, this pairing is likely to lead to problems, and in the event of a split, the separation is often acrimonious. Even if passion flows between you at the early stages of your relationship, you are not likely to be happy together in the long run.

Horse and Rat are better off not marrying or living together as partners. Even when there is love flowing back and forth during the initial stages, you are unlikely to be close over the long term. Note however that astrological opposites can coexist quite harmoniously as friends or siblings.

CURE: If a Horse is already married to a Rat, the solution to improve your prospects for lasting happiness is to introduce the secret friend of each other into your living space. This can be done through the symbolic use of figurines or art. As a pair, you should thus display the secret friend of the Rat, the **Ox**, and the secret friend of the Horse, the **Sheep**, in the home.

HORSE with RAT

In 2021, OK if you keep your distance

The Horse and Rat do not make compatible partners. You are natural adversaries, positioned directly opposite one another in the astrological wheel; but of the six pairs of adversaries, your acrimony with each other is the least pronounced. Indeed, some Horse and Rat pairings form extremely happy and lasting marriages or become the firmest of friends.

When there is compatibility between you, it usually has to do with some other ascendant in one of your charts. In general, Horse and Rat are rarely advised by any Chinese astrologer to seek out a future with one another where your lives intertwine too closely, because should you need to extricate, the separation will be long-winded and gruelling, leaving both with scars neither of you need.

In 2021, you enjoy a respite and the relationship between Horse and Rat improves. Both are blessed by *Big Auspicious* stars from the 24 Mountains, so both are headed towards big things. But Rat and Horse are unlikely to be headed towards the same thing. Your paths may travel in the same direction, but you are more likely on parallel planes that never meet. If you find yourselves in a relationship where both are happy with each other's success, but otherwise leave each other well alone, then you can superficially be good friends. But if you let yourselves get entangled in each other's affairs, it could get messy.

In romance, there is plenty of chemistry. Horse is the more amorous, and Rat quickly gets ensnared. Passionate one-night stands are not unusual between these two; but try to engage your emotions and the problems begin. The Rat is too practical for the Horse, and the Horse too free-spirited for the Rat.

When you talk on a grounded level, you do not share the same values. Discussing mutual goals will only lead Rat to conclude that the Horse is flighty and erratic, while Horse views Rat as tiresome and boring. Rat feels overly responsible for the Horse, unlikely to approve of the Horse's impetuous turns of hoof. Horse meanwhile feels shackled by the Rat's over-sensibilities.

As workmates however, the two of you can get along. Because your thought processes are so different, it can come across refreshing, even inspirational, when you exchange ideas. Your energies intertwine productively, so this year, if in a work or business relationship, you two can thrive. Just don't get too close.

CURE: To improve things between a Horse and Rat who are already together, you should each carry each other's secret friend. The Horse should carry an image of the **Ox**, and the Rat should carry an image of the **Sheep**.

HORSE with OX

Fabulous together in 2021

While Horse and Ox are as different as night and day, the energies each brings to the table in 2021 make this a very special team. The two combine to create a sum-of-ten, which brings completion luck, so this year this pair can achieve a lot together. A Horse and Ox working together in 2021 can scale great heights and achieve incredible successes, and the bigger they aim, the higher they can climb.

The Ox is stable and dependable, while the Horse is impulsive and courageous, and the individual traits of each, while very different, come together to create some real magic in this year of the Ox.

As a team, Horse and Ox have all the ingredients required to conjure up really great success. Their outcomes are blessed with triumph, and because individually both enjoy superb indications from their respective charts, there will be few blips and glitches along the way.

Ox's calm and steady nature keeps Horse's impetuousness in check, while Horse's bravado and daring breathes new life into the Ox. Together they become each other's secret ingredient for success.

In love, Horse awakens all that is passionate in the Ox, while Ox ensures Horse enjoys the security it craves. Horse may be spontaneous and rash, living life on the edge, but deep down is a sensible soul, and having an Ox partner provides the stability it needs to be as wild as it likes. Ox meanwhile learns to live life in full colour with a Horse mate at its side.

If these two are married, life at home is never dull. It is easy for them to agree on how they want to do things as a family. The Ox will usually be the main breadwinner, but the Horse is an equal partner in every sense of the word. They will rarely compete about who contributes more to the household, and both will give selflessly and gallantly.

At work, Horse and Ox find plenty of common ground in 2021. Their relationship this year will be characterised by enthusiasm, delight and an equal determination for success. They keep their eyes on the goal and will not allow each other to be side-tracked by the things that don't matter. But neither will be uptight about it.

A wonderful year ahead for this very promising pair!

HORSE with TIGER

Sum-of-ten amplifies an already fabulous union

A passionate pair of kindred spirits who fight and argue, then make up with intense humour. Both are impulsive, restless and energetic, and their personalities gel perfectly. They are free spirits unshackled by society's norms and expectations, and they fuel each other's thirst for adventure and lust for living. If they have the good fortune to meet and fall in love, their lives are blessed indeed!

The coming year makes this volcanic pairing erupt with good fortune! They not only bring each other unbridled passion but huge success and accomplishment also. 2021 sees their fortunes combine in the most spectacular of ways, forming a sum-of-ten that allows them to triumph in whatever joint endeavours they pursue.

> Whether Horse and Tiger are building a home, life or business together, they always have a wild ride doing so, and the energies of this year help them no end.

Tiger's flaming energy and Horse's big store of good fortune make them a pair that everyone will idealise. In many ways, their match is one made in heaven. The connection between them transcends the merely

physical; there is a very spiritual dimension to the connection. When Horse and Tiger get together, their aspirations are no longer superficial.

Horse and Tiger are also astrological allies, and together with the Dog, make up the "three adventurers" of the Chinese Zodiac. Resilience, courage and determination are attributes strongly associated with these signs, and when together, they bring out all these very positive traits in each other.

In 2021, Horse and Tiger find pure magic together. Tiger is likely to be the one pursuing the Horse, with completely honourable intentions. They inspire noble qualities in each other, bringing out goodness and inner kindness.

Their communication is almost intuitive. They share an easy camaraderie and a great sense of humour. They are also incredibly tolerant of each other and are likely to create a world of their own, strongly bonding with each other and staying supportive through life. This match has an excellent chance of lasting a long time. Their energies in 2021 are in perfect sync, and as a couple, this year could be one of their very best yet!

HORSE with RABBIT

Attraction grows in 2021

The Horse and Rabbit share a natural love bond. The Rabbit is the Peach Blossom Animal of the Horse, so attraction between these two comes very naturally. Even though their personalities and interests differ considerably, there is a special spark occurring between them which cannot be explained, especially in 2021.

In this pairing, Rabbit willingly follows the adventurous Horse on a joyride, and when together, fun and happiness flows effortlessly! Time spent together is never boring, and there is genuine devotion felt on both sides

> In 2021, the year's energies bring these two together. The Rabbit's Peach Blossom joining with the Horse's Victory Star conjures up a storm of love vibes. Passion flows freely with each sweeping the other off its feet!

2021 promises to be a wonderful time for a Horse and Rabbit pairing, especially so if they come together in a romantic setting. The Horse's energetic nature breathes life into the more sedate Rabbit, bringing out its passionate and carefree side. Around a Horse, Rabbit feels free and able to conquer the world. Horse meanwhile easily falls head over heels for the demure Rabbit, who oozes passion this year under the spell of the *Peach Blossom*.

> This union works especially well for those in the budding stages of the relationship. Those who have only just met have many adventures to look forward to together, and the attraction each feels for the other grows stronger through the year.

But for those who have been involved with each other for a while, they need to watch out for third parties who may interfere with their heady mix of romance. Temptation is everywhere, especially for the Rabbit, so for the pairing to last, Horse needs to stay devoted, interested and vigilant.

This year, the energies are strongly positive for these two, helping the relationship blossom and flourish, but when the year is over, whether they stay together or not depends on many other things. They may make a passionate pairing, but the attraction can be superficial. Unless there are common interests and goals, the fire may not burn quite so bright once the magic of 2021 comes to a close.

HORSE with DRAGON
This unlikely match
blessed by the heavens in 2021

Horse and Dragon may not make your most likely
match, but all this changes in 2021. The year brings
some magical energies the way of the Horse, who
becomes especially alluring to the mighty Dragon. The
Horse is a real winner in 2021 with the Victory Star on
its side, and also the blessings of the *Golden Deity*. If
a Horse catches the eye of a Dragon, the Dragon can
hardly resist.

In 2021, Horse & Dragon can look forward
to wonderful adventures together, with
Horse leading the charge. In love, there is
unbridled passion, and in work, both keep
the other motivated and driven.

So much good energy flows between a Horse and
Dragon this year. In this relationship, it is often
the Dragon who drives the relationship in terms of
viewpoint and agenda, but in 2021, Dragon is happy
to let Horse take the reins. These two signs are equally
impetuous, courageous and impulsive, but instead of
this being a recipe for disaster, they bring each other
plenty of excitement and success. They form strong
bonds in 2021, and if in a love relationship, they make
the sheets burn with passion.

This is not a year when their energies are well-matched. Dragon is stronger from an element luck perspective, while Horse is stronger with good flying stars. Horse has the added benefit of not one but two *Big Auspicious* stars. Together with a Dragon, Horse finds the courage and discipline to transform opportunities into success.

Theirs is a big picture approach and their worlds are coloured by long strokes of the paintbrush. Both relish challenges and have independent spirits that refuse to be restrained. Thus conventions and traditions never get in their way. They are a strongly supportive and loyal pair with never a dull moment.

Infidelities, if any, are swept into oblivion by the tide of their own passion for each other. Neither are the petty kind, so they can make blunder after blunder and still forgive and forget. For them, they understand that choices are not made in a void; and if in the process of a decision one hurts or slights the other, they will not hold a grudge as long as the hurt was unintentional. This gives the relationship incredible resilience, especially in an afflicted year when blunders will be made. A charming coupling where the pleasures outweigh any pain.

HORSE with SNAKE

Passion ignites between two Fire signs

The Horse will always find the Snake attractive, and vice versa. These are two Fire element individuals who are intense and passionate - but also very different. While they enjoy the same things on the surface, their heartbeats vibrate to different tunes.

The Horse is the ultimate adventurer of the Zodiac, able to up and take off at a moment's notice, a creature that hates to be shackled down. The Snake appreciates exploration, but requires more thought and planning. It can match the Horse for being impetuous and sudden, but its more traditional values prevents the Snake from "risking it all" with an impulsive moment of bravado.

While there is plenty of chemistry between Snake and Horse, they are unlikely to build a stable and long-lasting marriage together. They adore each other to bits but their approaches to life are simply too different.

More likely, a Horse and Snake can become best pals who take fantastic trips together, have a whole bundle of laughs, even become friends with benefits, but when it comes to real life, they are more likely to find it with another partner.

In a work situation, Horse and Snake gel very well. They bring different talents to the table, and because they genuinely enjoy each other's company, the process is always gratifying. Neither are bothered about who takes the credit, so they focus well on the tasks at hand. Neither have the need to hog the limelight, and so they work well as equal partners.

In 2021, Horse has superior feng shui indications, but these two signs share a *Big Auspicious* star with one another. This suggests that when they work together this year, they acheive not just moderate success but something quite phenomenal. However, it will be Horse benefitting the Snake more than the other way around this year.

With their respective luck patterns, it benefits any partnership they have with one another if the Horse takes charge, but Snake may not be overly thrilled by the prospect. If they come together romantically, there are thrills and delights galore, but if either starts to push for more commitment, the other may get frightened off. Horse and Snake share fabulous affinity, but this is only the case if neither expects too much of the other.

HORSE with HORSE

Two Horses make a winning pair in 2021

Two Horses can make the best of friends and the most passionate of lovers. This is one of the signs of the Zodiac which hits it off like a house on fire with another of its own sign. The Horse's spirited approach to life finds immediate gratification in the company of another Horse. Their mutual love for adventure allows them to seek out and find thrilling escapades together, and their similar attitudes lead them to form strong bonds with one another.

> 2021 sees the connection between two Horses strengthen. With the Victory Star squarely in their sector, flanked by two Big Auspicious and the Star of Golden Deity, two Horses not only share interests and diversions, they achieve much success together.

Their very special luck in 2021 serves to elevate their relationship to whole new levels. Whether they are already married, at the dating stage, working together or just very good friends, they inspire one another to significant highs and attainments. They may be going after a shared goal or pursuing their aspirations individually, but they become a solid source of support for one another through a very auspicious time.

When two Horses work together, they cooperate
well because there is no jealousy or judgement.
Their expectations are realistic, making them very
comfortable in each other's company. Tension does not
come into the picture because the Horse is the free spirit
of the Zodiac, and will rarely create drama for drama's
sake. So with another of its own sign, things always
stay relaxed, productive and buoyant.

Two Horses work especially well if they are pursuing
a passion project or a cause that is close to their hearts.
When they believe in something emotionally, they put
their whole hearts into it, and this year, when they try
that hard, phenomenal success is quite possible.

As lovers, two Horses burn up the sheets! They are
passion personified. Neither are the shy type in bed,
and with each other, sparks fly. A marriage between
two Horses can last because each can go their own
way without the other feeling insecure. Yet when they
come together, they always simmer with passion and so
much love.

HORSE with SHEEP

Intermittent hostility but emerging stronger

Although Horse and Sheep share an astrologically closely linked and deep relationship, in 2021 they could nevertheless experience verbal clashes with each other. While they have strong ties, the energies this year bring very quarrelsome energies the way of the Sheep, and these two share an intensely passionate rapport where everything gets enhanced.

Their feelings and emotions, when it has to do with each other, get magnified out of proportion, and whatever they feel, either positive or negative, they express tenfold to each other.

In 2021, it would appear that together or individually they have a lot of latent hostility energy to deal with. They need an extraordinary store of patience and plenty of goodwill to ride through a stormy year ahead. Even with strong feng shui cures in place, it is likely there will be intermittent hostility causing unhappiness and a great deal of aggravation.

FENG SHUI CURE: The way to smooth the year for this pair is to use the power of **Fire energy** and to **wear red** as much as possible.

Horse and Sheep have the ability to make each other extremely happy. They think in the same way and are also physically very compatible. They are able to please each other and to establish good foundations for long-term happiness. Their attraction is rooted in their attitudes which complement each other.

The Zodiac is bullish about a Horse and Sheep pairing as this couple are not just secret friends but also soulmates. They share the same Zodiac House, that of sexuality and passion, with Horse exuding the male yang energy and Sheep creating the female yin energy. This translates to suggest complete and utter compatibility. They have a special relationship that is strong and enduring that can last the long haul. The Horse is upfront and courageous and the Sheep is constant and stable. The Horse likes to lead and take charge, and this is just fine with the gentle, easy-going Sheep. Between them is a huge store of goodwill.

2021 may mess up their passionate and idyllic existence a little, as tempers tend to flare, but a Horse and Sheep will always make up quickly after a fight, and this makes them even stronger. There is no doubt that Horse and Sheep can build a very happy and successful marriage or partnership together, even if this year may not be their best one.

HORSE with MONKEY

So much fun together!

A match comprising Horse and Monkey brings together two of the Zodiac's mesmerizing signs. Physically, the two could not be more different and temperamentally too. Merging them together is an impossible task as it would be like trying to merge the wind with the sun.

The Horse is as fiery as the wind, although it can also be as tender as the light morning breeze. The Monkey is the sun - radiant, brilliant and glowing with its bright intellect and incredible cunning. Yet to describe them as diametrical opposites would not be doing them justice.

What brings them together and makes them compatible is the acute similarity of their expectations – from life, friends, colleagues and from each other! Both are natural leaders able to lead battalions onto the battlefield. Their modus operandi differ but ultimately, they reach the same conclusions.

Should they find each other, they could quite literally love each other to death, for one will inspire the other to great heights. In this pairing, Horse brings a natural vitality that is endearing to the Monkey. Monkey in 2021 has outstanding element luck, with some sensational successes coming its way, and with a Horse by its side, every success gets magnified.

What could be the only snag in this relationship is Monkey's more quarrelsome nature this year, but because Horse has a lot of tolerance for someone it is enamoured with, this will not stop a passionate love affair from blooming once it gets going.

When Horse and Monkey come together in love, they last not only because there is genuine attraction but also genuine respect. They are both naturally friendly personalities, enjoying each other's company but also making a fabulous "It" Couple. The home they build together will transform into some kind of clubhouse for their mutual friends, and they have equal fun entertaining others as they do after the party is over. And the afterparty is sensational!

2021 sees both of these signs headed for very good years, so there is no need for either to "prop up" the other. Both stand on their own two feet making this a partnership of equals, but one with a lot of love and laughter.

HORSE with ROOSTER
Building an exciting future together

Horse and Rooster have an incredibly restful affinity, so they are really very good for one another. Here we see two signs whose personalities may not be similar, but each possess attributes that appeal to the other. And with both enjoying an active and auspicious year when their chi levels are high, there is genuine attraction between them. They can come together in a love relationship or bring out the best in each other in a business partnership. Whatever the nature of their union, these two create amazing synergy together.

In 2021, Horse has the Victory Star and Rooster has the Wealth Star. Their luck patterns sync up fabulously to make a powerful couple, and because their energies are so aligned, their compatibility gets enhanced.

The Horse is the adventurer in the relationship, but Rooster matches Horse in terms of a willingness to take a risk. The difference is that Rooster will tend to be the more grounded of the two, so it will be the sensible one in the relationship. Horse meanwhile encourages the Rooster to live and love life. The Rooster is a passionate creature at heart but needs the right partner to really let loose. And with a Horse, the Rooster finds this.

If Rooster and Horse meet and fall for each other this year, they could fall hard indeed. Both are going through great years in terms of luck. If they pursue a relationship together, they are doing so in the best setting possible.

Because their professional lives are going well, they do not have to worry about much, so when they indulge in romance, they are completely there. There is no stress and there are no emergencies to cloud the picture.

As colleagues or business partners, Horse and Rooster work well because Horse is willing to let the domineering Rooster take charge. Horse submits to Rooster not because it is not its equal, but because it respects the Rooster so much. Rooster meanwhile will not take Horse for granted, perfectly recognising Horse's contribution.

In a marriage, there is a balanced mix of passion and sensibility in the pairing. The Horse brings plenty of fire while the Rooster provides the inspiration. This is a pairing that can last the long haul.

HORSE with DOG

Two individuals motivated by the same things

Horse and Dog are astrological allies of the Zodiac, so they are good for each other no matter the year or circumstance. A Horse and Dog who get married will build a fabulous family life together. Both stay very domesticated in their thinking no matter how busy they get outside of the home. Both are family-oriented individuals who have plenty of time for the family.

In 2021, Dog has the afflictive loss star, but with a Horse partner by its side, there is nothing Dog cannot weather. Horse brings Dog courage and perseverance no matter the obstacle.

Between Horse and Dog, there always flows a lot of understanding and love. These two signs find it easy to share ideas and assets, and they go through good times and bad with the same spirit of give and take. They have the same kind of humour and are able to walk through difficult challenges in the best of spirits.

They generate powerful synergy to take advantage of whatever opportunities open up for them. In a year when the Horse enjoys not one but two *Big Auspicious* stars, and the Dog has a *Small Auspicious*, they make a dynamic and promising duo indeed.

They are socially popular and will find they like the same types of people. Horse and Dog generate good hype as a couple and as a result, their social life is excellent. Both are extroverts by nature. They are good at making friends and transforming business associates into life-long allies. Their great strength is in networking. If they run a business together, they collaborate excellently.

These are two people motivated by high ideals. They cherish the same values so there is an inner bonding that brings them closer with each passing year. They get fired up and relentlessly pursue causes they believe in. They think alike with neither being overly sensitive or given to looking to blame the other should things go wrong.

They act out of impulse so there is usually no heavy discussion of serious issues between them. Their interactions are rarely if ever tense, and they are happy to do away with formality. These are instant decision makers and rightly or wrongly, they are happy to bumble their way through life, be their own counsel and create their own inspiration.

HORSE with BOAR

An easy-going pairing

While Horse and Boar have no special affinity, they have what it takes to form a loving and lasting relationship with one another. They personify the essence of their respective elements - Fire and Water - being direct opposites in both appearance and personality, with one fast and fiery, the other slow and steady.

> But put these two together and they can live and work together amicably with great success and happiness. Over time, they develop a special kind of respect and tolerance for one another's foibles.

Their compatibility arises as much from the good-natured sensitivity of the Boar, who is generally extremely easy-going, as from the steadfast loyalty of the Horse. Despite any number of temper tantrums, Horse and Boar always kiss and make up. These two do not hold grudges.

In 2021, Horse has far better luck than Boar, so it will be the Horse that props up the both of them. The Boar unfortunately suffers the Loss Star, which can manifest in money loss or some other way; but with a Horse by its side, the Boar does not just "survive" but positively thrives. The Horse meanwhile finds the Boar a steadying force in its life. The Horse goes through a year when it is all systems go, and if left unchecked, could run itself right off the rails. But with a Boar partner, it keeps its feet on the ground.

Horse is a restless impulsive creature, while Boar tends to be more circumspect and careful, usually thinking things through before acting. Sometimes Boar comes across too slow and indecisive to the Horse, but they always agree to meet halfway and common sense prevails, so the relationship works well most of the time.

They are comfortable with each other and not too demanding; their interactions are civil, and any arguments rarely descend into shouting matches. This is a balanced union where giving and taking is well-shared between the two.

As business partners, they provide just the right mix of *yin* and *yang* to form a creative and productive partnership. As work colleagues, they are not competitive with one another, so they can become true allies and even good friends. In love and marriage, they make a cozy couple with no fear that one or the other will stray - no passionate fireworks but with enough excitement to sustain a healthy and lasting marriage.

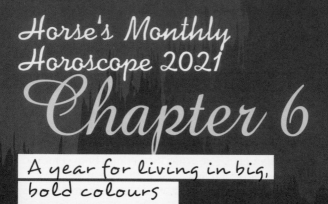

Horse's Monthly Horoscope 2021

Chapter 6

A year for living in big, bold colours

The Horse is supremely lucky this year! You enjoy extremely auspicious indications, with two Big Auspicious Stars and a Golden Deity Star backing you. The Victory Star meanwhile makes you a winner in everything you do.

A year to live in big, bold colours; one where you can truly follow your dreams. If you feel passionately about something, the causes and conditions will surely come together to help you achieve all of your goals. For you, no mountain is too big to climb if the will is there. A year to enjoy whether you are chasing success, looking for love or seeking general happiness.

1st Month
February 4th - March 5th 2021

....

STARTING THE YEAR RIGHT WITH THE SUM-OF-TEN

Everything goes right for the Horse. You may have been sitting on some ideas for a while, and as the new year unfolds, opportunities to turn those ideas into reality come thick and fast. Whether a job offer, a helping hand lent by the right connections, or in the form of funding, you get to pursue your dreams. If you have something you've been wanting to do, don't wait too long. Your luck this year starts off very well so don't waste this time procrastinating. Even if you don't think you are quite ready, start taking your first steps. Let everything come together for you as you take action. If you need everything to be perfect before you are willing to start, you won't get started.

....

Work & Career - *Taking on more*

Your energy levels are running at full throttle, so this is the time to get things done! You are in the position to take on more responsibilities, so you should offer to do so. Expand your horizons and don't work in a cocoon. See the forest for the trees as everything falls into perspective for you. Even as you take on more and more, focus on quality rather than quantity. You can achieve both but don't let quality suffer because you are doing more. You are mentally sharp, and it is easy for you to grasp what really matters in any situation. Your strategic thinking goes up a notch. Be confident when sharing views and opinions; if you project confidence, others will have confidence in you. You also enjoy completion luck, so it won't take you ages to finish projects or meet your targets. Use this time to get ahead of the pack whatever your work environment. Some of you could get promoted this month.

> A high energy period when your enthusiasm attracts others of similar energy into your orbit.

Business - *Publicity blitz*

Not much goes wrong for the Horse this month. The entrepreneurs among you thrive in high profile environments, so welcome any publicity you can get. If fame helps you in your business, actively court it. For now, any publicity is good publicity, so don't worry too much when it comes to image. Be yourself, follow your instincts, be bold when taking risks. This is the ideal time to begin an advertising campaign or to go on a publicity blitz, as everyone seems under your spell. Take full advantage when others offer you help - whether in money or in kind. Opportunities to get your message out there fall into your lap with minimal effort. Horses are impetuous characters and this month, that impetuousness comes across extremely attractive! Put that charisma to good use to win others onto your side, to gain you new customers, and to help your brand or business flourish!

> **ENHANCER FOR THE MONTH:** Boost fame and publicity luck with the **Black Tortoise Lunar Mansions Enhancer.** Activating your Lunar Mansions helps you get your timing right, and ensures that the opportunities meant for you come your way in guises where you can make the most of them.

Love & Relationships - *Passion runs high*

A very romantic time for the Horse when passion runs high! Enjoy the month but don't let yourself get carried away. Single Horses stand a good chance to find someone to pique their interest beyond first dates. But those already in a relationship need to beware the *External Flower of Romance.* Don't cheat on your partner or do something you will regret. Protect what you have with the **Enhancing Relationships Talisman.**

School & Education - *Seeking the limelight*

Basking in the limelight comes naturally to the Horse this month, so if the spotlight is not currently on you, you find yourself actively seeking it. You can be a huge star if that's what you want - but go after it with substance. Whatever you're trying to excel in, put in the work, and the rest will follow!

2nd Month
March 6th - April 4th 2021

PROSPERITY STAR PAYS A VISIT

Another wonderful month for the Horse! Your good fortune from last month continues to ripen, so good things continue to happen for you! You can take risks and for sure can indulge in some lavish personal pampering! An auspicious month when living it up will not harm you one bit but will actually enhance and push in even more good chi, as happy, luxurious events can attract more money luck! A good time to plan for the truly big things in your life, like marriage, moving house, changing job, signing new deals etc. Your karma is in full swing but to have it work for you, you should do some charity work or donate to worthwhile causes. The more you give, the more you receive!

Work & Career - *Good support*

You already enjoyed some doses of good luck last month, but this month your luck really overflows! You have support from all the right quarters and important people appreciate your good qualities and talents. A good time to take a look at your career path and discuss with your boss if appropriate. There are exciting developments in the pipeline. If there's something you would like to be involved in, speak up. You are a valued member of the team and your enthusiasm is well appreciated. If asked to take on tasks you are unfamiliar with, view it as a challenge and an opportunity to show your proficiency; but more than that, your good attitude.

Fabulous money luck, and for some of you, a windfall. A time when you can take some risks.

Business - *Eloquent*

Business luck is excellent making this a good time to start new projects, sign agreements, join forces with a promising partner, launch a new product... Also a fruitful time to engage in important discussions, as you are eloquent and capable of influencing others over to your way of thinking. Your fortunes are looking up and others are attracted to your good chi. If you need to approach someone for a favour, go ahead. It is hard for anyone to refuse you this month!

You may want to help out a friend by giving them some business. If the amount is insignificant, do what you like, but don't risk a friendship by awarding a job when you know they are not the right person. It may be better to make an excuse than fall into major disagreements later on.

186

Love & Relationships - *Spoilt for choice*

Singles are spoilt for choice if looking to get hitched. There are multiple suitors waiting in the sidelines, so you can be as picky as you like. Don't rush into anything unless you are sure. Committing to someone for the sake of being in a relationship could cause you miss out on something really special that's about to come along. Hold out on your heartstrings till you know for sure you've found your soul mate.

Education - *Work-play balance*

Your social life is packed! And it may not be with your usual group of friends. You find it easy to strike up new acquaintances who quickly become best buddies. Mixing with new people could well be the tonic you need now. Academic work goes well, but balancing it out with a healthy social life can only be good for you.

> **ENHANCER FOR THE MONTH:** Carry the **Asset Bull Wealth Amulet** to activate the prosperity star of the month. This increases your chances of spotting the best deals and making intelligent investment plays that end up significantly augmenting your net worth. Those starting a new business benefit from carrying the **White Tiger Constellation Lucky Charms**.

White Tiger Constellation Lucky Charms

3rd Month
April 5th - May 5th 2021

....

DANGER OF DUPLICITY

This month brings risk of being cheated, taken for a ride or even getting physically mugged. Being robbed is a possibility and financial loss can come in a variety of guises. Avoid late nights as the hours past midnight are your most vulnerable, so if out and about, take extra care. Use the long, boring route rather than short cuts that pass through dark lanes or empty stretches of abandoned land.

Do not put yourself in danger by getting into risky situations. If there is a fight and you are a bystander, leave the scene. For females, innocent flirtations may be misunderstood. The less you spread your social wings, the better. It is safer to keep a low profile and concentrate on work!

....

Work & Career - *Beware workplace politics*

The office seems fraught with petty squabbles and some rivalry may drag you down and depress you. You aren't in the mood to fight back, so just be savvy and keep your eyes and ears open. Don't become a victim of office politics. By playing your cards right, you can emerge unscathed or even triumphant without open hostility towards your rivals. They may not know what or who hits them! This month it is wiser to hold your tongue than say something sharp or sarcastic which can be used against you later. Keep your thoughts to yourself and don't confide in anyone however close they may seem. If you say the wrong thing, they could fall on the wrong ears. Work smart rather than hard, but your natural charm and easy manners will be of great help!

Not a time to splurge. Unexpected expenses may crop up which puts a strain on your cash flow.

Business - *Take a back seat*

Better to be a back-seat passenger than driver or navigator. Your luck is down so let others be on the front line or in the line of fire so to speak! Your fellow directors or staff may have better luck than you, so ride on their good luck rather than depend on your own. Don't take risks when it comes to money. A bad month for starting anything new, expanding your workforce, or taking on new partners. Avoid new initiatives, and best not to sign anything that the courts have jurisdiction over. If you can maintain the status quo, you should consider yourself lucky! Avoid wildcat schemes and focus on building knowledge. This is a time for stillness, patience and preparation. No need to make decisions on things you are not ready to decide on. Hold off till next month when your luck improves.

Love & Relationships - *Beware*

Those young and single are more vulnerable and must be wary. Your sex appeal may attract all the wrong suitors with dishonourable intentions! And instead of being accosted in some dark, sleazy place, such advances and unsavoury offers may actually come from your workplace! You have a lot of natural charm but that allure seems to be baiting all the wrong men, so just be extra careful. Married Horses will be more interested in their career or social life than in their marriage. Every relationship goes through its ups and downs, that's natural. But don't neglect your partner to the extent they begin to look elsewhere for what they need.

Education - *Stay conscientious*

Be prepared for unexpected obstacles that pop up. Though things may not be smooth sailing and a tempest may well be brewing, you can sail through if you put your mind to it. The hardworking among you will prevail and even excel.

ENHANCER FOR THE MONTH: Carry the Rhino and Elephant **Anti-Robbery Amulet** to protect against money loss. Protect your marriage with the **Enhancing Relationships Amulet**.

Anti-Robbery Amulet

4th Month
May 6th - June 5th 2021

HO TU FOR ACCUMULATING KNOWLEDGE

A month when not only do you grow as a person, you also look at the world differently, as if from an elevated level. You become more philosophical and begin to see life from new perspectives. You benefit from newfound wisdom which allows you to see the wood for the trees. Those pursuing knowledge gain it easily; you read the right books and meet up with the right teachers. Your confidence grows, making you more assured that the choices you make are the right ones. The arrival of the *Heaven Star* provides an invisible guiding force, and weans you off having to ask for too many opinions before deciding on something. The Horse in school or college particularly benefits from the energies of the month.

Work & Career - *Powerful people helping you*

An exciting time for the Horse climbing the career ladder. There are people in powerful places helping you, whether directly or behind the scenes. Your relationship with your boss improves, and the support of your superiors propels you ahead. If given more responsibilities, accept and step up. Avoid being calculative when it comes to remuneration. The less greedy you are, the more you'll end up getting. This month you should consider every opportunity to work harder a blessing. Your Ho Tu indicates that whatever you start now bears lasting fruit.

ENHANCER FOR THE MONTH: Carry the **Ho Tu Enhancer** for this very special luck to ripen for you. Activating the Ho Tu in your chart brings intelligence, wisdom and better instincts. You gain confidence, because when you make decisions, you are confident of those decisions. Because your luck is good, this deep self-assurance only serves to augment all the opportunities and goodies coming your way.

Business - *Making friends easily*

If thinking of expanding, you can move confidently forward. You have growth luck, and the more ambitious you are, the bigger your results. Doors open; you only have to knock. A fruitful time to be persistent in your networking. If there is someone you want to meet, put in more effort and you could be bosom pals in no time. The Horse is always charming, but this month you are also extremely easy to connect with. Allow your natural personality free rein and you will surprise even yourself. This month you also get a lot closer to those who work for you. Engage your colleagues in conversations that go beyond the work. Bonds made now grow stronger over time.

Love & Relationships - *Spouse a big help*

Romance luck enters, giving you have the upper hand in relationships. But you also possess the charm to hide this fact from your conquest; this is what makes you so irresistible! The single Horse is sure to get lucky! How serious a relationship you want is up to you, but the Horse always goes with the flow, allowing its partner to dictate the pace. If married, your luck now is stronger than ever, so make the most of your attached status.

Home & Family - *Hospitable*

Your home is particularly welcoming now so play host and organize a party! Your personal energy is up and running and inviting others to share that with you enhances your energy and mood further.

Education - *Nothing wrong with spoonfeeding*

Life becomes significantly easier when someone older and wiser takes the reins and guides you towards success. Some call it "spoon-feeding" but why not! If you are lucky enough to have someone who takes such close interest in your scholastic career, make the most of it!

5th Month
June 6th - July 6th 2021

MISFORTUNE STAR ARRIVES.
STAY WARY.

The Five Yellow enters the picture making the coming month less than agreeable. You can expect obstacles to success in the most well-oiled of projects and endeavours. Take it in your stride because this is just a temporary blip in your luck. Use this period to consolidate and take stock. If you are unsure of something, see it as a sign to take pause. Restrain your natural tendency to impetuousness and rein in that instinctive bravado of your sign. Make friends not enemies and be uncontroversial with your actions and words. Not the best month of the year, but surely not a terrible one either.

Work & Career - *Don't be rash*

Others find it more difficult relating to you because you read too much into everything that's said and done. Don't allow this to create a rift between yourself and your workmates. The last thing you need now is to be freezed out. Try to see the positive side of everything that is said to you. Don't get overly affected by the comments of others, some of which may be said in jest.

Those with thicker skins will get through the month better, more happily and more successfully.

A month to lie low. Do not make big decisions without thinking things through. Much better to save big choices for another time.

Business - *Lie low*
The misfortune star plays havoc with your emotions, so refrain from making important moves that matter. Your judgement may be off, so take good advice rather than try to work everything out yourself. Avoid important discussions and do not sign off on important documents. Business ventures started now are likely to be flawed, so plan, but wait before taking action. This may be a good time to take a holiday! Could be just what you need to prevent your afflicted luck rubbing off on your business ventures. Emergency issues may arise which you have to deal with, but whatever can be delayed till next month should be.

Love & Relationships - *Don't be so serious!*
Petty quarrels with your partner could leave you feeling rather sorry for yourself. When you disagree over something, don't react impulsively. Before responding in a way you regret, take time to clear your head. Don't take anything personally. For now it is better to let the other side win when it comes to disagreements. If

you're prepared to concede even if you believe you are right, you end up a lot happier and your relationship benefits. Fix arguments quickly because you don't want something to fester and risk either of you confiding the wrong things to the wrong people. Remember - the *external star of romance* hovers through the air this year, and infidelities are eminently possible. Carry the **Enhancing Relationships Amulet** or wear the **Marriage Saver Medallion** if you feel your relationship is in this kind of danger.

Education - *Prepare early*

If feeling under the weather, give yourself time to get better rather than press on and risk getting more sick. Not a good month to sit for exams, but if you don't have a choice, your priority should be to get enough rest, so you give yourself every chance to do your best with a clear mind. Last minute mugging will not work now. If you are in exam month, the best strategy is to prepare much earlier.

CURE FOR THE MONTH: Carry the **Five Element Pagoda with Tree of Life Amulet** and place a miniature pagoda on your work desk.

6th Month
July 7th - Aug 7th 2021

FRIENDSHIPS BLOSSOM. LOVE BLOOMS!

Your luck rebounds in a big way! The coming month sees all manner of relationships flourish for the Horse. A time when you can develop your friendships and deepen your bonds, whether romantic, platonic or work-related. Your natural charm returns and others can hardly resist when you make an effort. Use this time to enjoy your social life, find the love of your life, and foster a stronger and more complete network of contacts and acquaintances. The month also favours students and those of you working at acquiring new knowledge. Discoveries and breakthroughs come for those engaged in research, and for some of you, spiritual epiphanies.

Work & Career - *Uncovering your talents*

Those in jobs where your skills of communication are sought after will feel much more at home than those involved in overly meticulous or monotonous work. You are bursting with ideas and craving something to engage your whole being. Your mind is constantly on the go, and if you don't have something to sink your teeth into, other distractions are bound to creep in. Share your ideas freely. If you can contribute more in the workplace, do so. No need to feel intimidated. This is a time when your true talents get uncovered and appreciated.

Business - Team-building

Everything will be about relationships and how well you forge them. An excellent time to make new connections. Your talent at networking could hook you some very lucrative deals. Don't stay low profile; make your presence felt! For the Horse this month, going after what you want is the way to get it. Important meetings are your forte as discussions go the way you plan and all you need is steer them in the desired direction! You show extraordinary skills in persuading others to see your views and agree with your suggestions. For business success, everything hinges on how well you put your ideas to work and how good you are at putting the various components together. Building reliable teams where everyone stands to gain is the best way to conquer what you're after.

Those of you in the driver's seat, think smart and exploit the talents of those around you. A few members of your team may have unrecognized abilities that can greatly aid your causes.

ENHANCER FOR THE MONTH: Boost your formidable skills in networking with the **Popularity Scarf**, and tap the luck of allies by displaying your Astrological Allies (the **Tiger** and **Dog**) on **Wishfulfilling Pillars** on your desk in front of you. Giving a leg up to this aspect of luck this month opens all kinds of doors for you.

Love & Relationships - *Be free!*

Your love life takes center stage! You may have some steadfast ideologies of how a romance should develop and these may actually have hampered you in the past. This month all this flies out the window and you find yourself enjoying yourself so much more! Be free, uninhibited and just go with the flow! No need to follow stuffy ideas because it really isn't you! So much love awaits the Horse this month, so allow yourself room to live life!

Education - *Like a sponge*

Luck strongly favours the Horse pursuing its studies this month! Knowledge gained now gets firmly entrenched for use later on, and not just for exams. Make the best use of your time to learn new things. Don't confine yourself to the syllabus. If you're still young, you're like a sponge. Use every opportunity to improve yourself and invite in all that life has to offer.

7th Month
Aug 8th - Sept 7th 2021

QUARRELSOME ENERGIES MAKE YOU DIFFICULT

Last month was all about your charm but the Quarrelsome Star emerges to wreck all that now. You find yourself irritable for no apparent reason, and if you don't pick fights with others, they pick them with you. Control your temper and don't let yourself get wound up over things that don't matter. Wear a lot of **the colour red** if you can. Don't be lured into a fight. There is risk of lawsuits and trouble with the law; if you find yourself in that kind of bind, don't get overconfident. Your luck is down and you cannot win no matter how clever you think you are. Lie low. Learn to relax and chill out. Those who have the privilege of taking a sabbatical or summer holiday, it could be the best thing for you now.

....

Work & Career - *Stay low profile*

Your difficult mood follows you to the workplace and sees you arguing frequently with colleagues. Try not to be disagreeable just because your temper takes you that way. Those not so close to you will not tolerate nearly as much as your own family would. For those in competitive work environments, rivals could use this weakness to their advantage. Don't let yourself play into their hands. The less in control you are of your emotions, the more vulnerable you'll be. When it comes to working within teams, there is no need to stand out. Right now it is better to keep a low profile.

Business - *Beware litigation*

Lawsuits become a risk when the #3 star appears. Make sure you have a good lawyer or you could miss something. When entering into any kind of contract, have everything down on paper to minimize misunderstandings later on. Differences in opinion may upset the working relationship between you and someone you liaise closely with. Business partnerships may go sour unless you are willing to eat humble pie and give in to some of the other party's demands. If they are not too unreasonable, you should do so. Avoid confrontations; if you think something is not right and you have no proof, give the benefit of doubt.

Use resources wisely; you don't have that much to depend on, so be judicious and don't overextend your limits. Despite the irritations, you have wealth luck. You just need to tap it!

Love & Relationships - *Don't try too hard*

Single Horses should not to try too hard when it comes to dating; you won't succeed and could end up looking desperate. The ones you are interested in could be put off. This month, persistence does not pay off, so stop banging your head on the wall. Those already in a relationship - don't let minor disagreements explode into big quarrels. If you insist on standing your ground and fighting for your rights, you may end up the loser.

Friendships - *Strained*
Friendships get strained because you hit misunderstanding after misunderstanding. Prepare for some arguments and bickerings. Things improve once the month is up. Don't let differences create a permanent rift.

Education - *No need to be perfect*
Horses pursuing their studies may suffer from mental blocks. Don't obsess over getting everything perfect. You need to start somewhere. If you spend your whole time planning, completing assignments could prove difficult. Get started, then improve from there.

CURE FOR THE MONTH: The Horse needs the **Apple Peace Amulet** and should wear more of **the colour red** this month to counter the ill effects of the #3 star.

8th Month
Sept 8th - Oct 7th 2021

LETHARGY SETS IN. NO MOOD FOR ANYTHING.

Another challenging month for the Horse, but this time not from your difficult mood, simply from your lack of enthusiasm and energy! The Illness Star shows up, sapping you of energy and putting a dampener on your plans. You become more susceptible to falling sick, so if you have prior health issues, do take extra care. Do NOT sleep in the South this month if ill health is a major worry for you. Look after yourself. Don't do things you don't feel up to. There is no need to be Mr or Miss Sociable. Don't let your pals bully you into going out, hanging out or doing anything you're uncomfortable with. You can reclaim your popularity crown later - for now, listen to what your body is telling you.

Work & Career - *Beware careless work*
Work becomes tedious because you're just so lacking in energy. Try to improve your efficiency, because endless hours pounding on at the same thing are what will make you careless and wear you down. It may just be a matter of time management, so take time to think about this and plan. Don't compromise on quality in your

haste to finish things off. Get used to working slow and steady - you could end up saving time this way while avoiding unnecessary mistakes. If you are finding deadlines hard to meet, discuss with your boss or team rather than churning out sub-standard work. Take work home rather than staying too late at the office.

Don't overwork as you may not realize you are burning out till you find out you have no more wick left to burn. A balanced life should be your goal this month; don't be too ambitious.

Business - Rely more on the team
Obstacles arise that although small affect your frame of mind. Difficulty focusing makes it hard to make good decisions. Keep this is a quiet month and avoid big changes in direction or working style. Don't try anything radical. When managing your team, allow them to make their own decisions and yes, even their own mistakes. This month, meddling too much won't bring any benefits. Be generous where credit is due. Let someone below you have their day; you will be remembered later. A hidden or seldom used talent can be used to great advantage, so exploit this skill to the max; you will be pleased with the results.

Love & Relationships - Erratic
Your love life gets rather erratic with unexpected

twists and turns. Avoid overreacting to situations or sensationalizing things; it might make for short term excitement but not for your long term frame of mind. Those in relationships have a comfortable rapport with your partner, but if still at the dating stage, your unpredictable behaviour could be off-putting. The more grounded you keep yourself, the better luck you will have when making a new relationship work.

Home & Family - *Nurturing*

Your family is supportive and always there for you, so make an effort. A small gesture like taking them out for dinner, bringing food home or contributing a new piece of furniture to the home will work wonders. Doing more for the family now gets paid back multiple times, and care from family members who are unconditional in loving you is the best antidote against the trials and tribulations of life.

Education - *Slow and steady*

Slow and steady wins the race. You may be lacking energy and motivation, so don't force yourself to slave away for others. Keep your study sessions short and manageable, but schedule in enough of them!

CURE FOR THE MONTH: Carry **Medicine Buddha's Mantra Wand** to boost your immunity and energy levels.

9th Month
Oct 8th - Nov 6th 2021

....

DOUBLE VICTORY. DOUBLE THE FUN. FEELING INVINCINBLE.

Your luck finally turns around and as you enter the last quarter of the year, you are in for a run of good luck! The *Victory Star* lends you invaluable support, allowing all your other good fortune indications to win out. You have lady luck on your side, so this is the time to forge strongly ahead with any passions and plans that you have. You have a competitive advantage over your rivals, so don't get intimidated by a little competition. Also a good time to embark on new endeavours and to change direction if you must. Some of you will enjoy windfall luck. But remember - the secret to lasting success is to be generous with your winnings. If you do well, be gracious. Enjoy the unseen hand of heaven helping you along, but always remember to give thanks and give back.

....

Work & Career - *Instincts are spot on*

A month when you enjoy good intuition, helping you to see what's really important. Your boss appreciates your big picture approach, and the more praise lavished on you, the better you do. Don't hold back when it comes to revealing your talents. Have total confidence in yourself. If you believe in whatever you are proposing, others will also; but if you appear hesitant, they take their cue from you. A promising month for the Horse, so make the most of it by striding ahead with purpose. There is no room for false modesty. The key to success will be your self-confidence and decisiveness.

> You begin to see things differently and for what they are, so this can be a brand new start. Things and people change; foes become friends and vice-versa!

Business - *Good publicity*

Business luck is strong. In contrast to last month when it was difficult to make good decisions, this month your instincts are spot on. If there is something new you want to try, go ahead. Be as creative as you want. New ideas hatched now have every chance of success. You also have enviable competition luck, so this is a good time to think about expanding market share. The best way to enhance your luck is with the **Desktop Flag of Victory** in the South of your office, or place on your work desk, or carry as an amulet hanging.

You get good publicity and your name becomes more hallowed. If you have to play the role of a public figure, go ahead and grant interviews to the media and meet the necessary people. Your PR skills are revving up and you can trust yourself to say all the right things.

Love & Relationships - *Vitality*

A newfound vitality finds you. You seem to have the energy of two people and begin to enjoy life tremendously. You experience satisfaction in the best way possible since have the right partner. Bliss is the word to describe you now. Explore new things as a couple and be dazzled by new experiences you never bothered with before. You can take the lead or be a humble follower; both scenarios end in your benefit. Keep an open mind and you will elevate yourself to new heights.

Education - *Many talents*

Winning comes easily, so competition suits you. You are blessed with enhanced leadership talents which you should put to good use. Don't focus just on studies; use this time to grow in other ways as well. If you are of two minds about something, go with what you think is best for you. Whether changing a subject or major, you are allowed to change your mind since the stars are on your side. If undecided, consult someone wiser whom you have always trusted. Such a mentor or confidante will banish all indecision and confusion from your system.

ENHANCER FOR THE MONTH: Carry the **Victory Banner Success Amulet** to make the most of your luck this month.

10th Month
Nov 7th - Dec 6th 2021

PLANNING FOR THE FUTURE

Another great month following on from a good one last month. This is the time to stay on track while planning for the future. Stay long term in your goals while pursuing short-term ones. There are many more good things in store, and they won't all come this month. This is the time to enjoy the journey and to view every victory as a stepping stone to even more spectacular wins down the road. Don't be satisfied with merely moderate success. You have so much potential this year, and this potential only burgeons as you close out the year. You're in great spirits because most things are going nicely in your favor, so your social and love life benefit.

Work & Career - *Lasting impressions*

You have a lot on your plate, but work is stimulating, so you won't mind putting in extra hours or sacrificing the odd weekend. Your creativity levels are through the roof and you have a lot to contribute, especially those in industries requiring original thought. An extremely fulfilling month if you have the freedom to define your own job scope. Be uncompromising when showing off your talents if you want the right people to notice. The impression you make now lasts a long time, so it is well worth the effort to go all out to impress. Don't be afraid to come across forward; if you back up your assertiveness with substance, you'll be forgiven anything.

Business - *Entering a new league*

Other months may have been about technical excellence, this month is about flair and originality. If you can capture the imagination of your market, you can make the leap into a whole new league! Use this time to make a mark that won't easily be forgotten. Your most lucrative efforts now will come from building contacts and developing relationships. Wealth luck is promising though the big time is still to come. Happily, it should be the near future. Best advice now is to keep setting interim targets and goals. Devise a comprehensive roadmap to success. Having indicative targets along the way will not just ensure you stay on course; it will boost morale to a degree that helps you accelerate the process.

> Luck is strong and much of the gains you experience will be a direct result of your efforts in building and strengthening all your relationships. Continue to put enough weight on this aspect of business.

Love & Relationships - *Great for singles!*

Those single among you have the best time, more so when this year seems filled with people attracted to you!

If not yet attached, you find yourself immersed in all sorts of delightful situations. Enjoy the dating game! You are in great demand so you might as well savour the moments, even if your true love may not be among this crop. Those married however must be careful of a third party spoiling a stable relationship. There is risk of infidelity, and this could come from either you or your spouse. Don't think you are immune to the advances of an outside party turning on the charm and lavishing you with praise and flattery. Don't let a moment's weakness to wreck things for you.

Education - *Growing up*

Any worries you have about shifting interpersonal dynamics within your friendship circles is unfounded. If you've been feeling displaced by a new member of the group, seize back your power and reclaim your role in the integral core of the group. But that's only if you want to. You could find yourself outgrowing that particular group because you yourself are changing.

> **ENHANCER FOR THE MONTH:** The Horse enjoys very auspicious sum-of-ten luck this month. Activate this superb indication by carrying the **Sum-of-Ten Enhancer**. This allows all your projects to come to successful conclusion and for all plans to succeed.

11th Month
Dec 7th - Jan 5th 2022

A FABULOUS END TO THE YEAR!
WEALTH, WINDFALL & HAPPINESS!

The year closes with the current prosperity star showing up, bringing very meaningful wealth luck into your life. Being year end, it is extra auspicious! For some, this could indicate a windfall or big bonus. Remember that the best way to tap one's luck is to activate it, so do make sure you surround yourself with wealth enhancers! Seize the opportunities coming your way while staying conscientious at work. The more effort you put in, the greater your rewards. The #8 star not only brings money luck but also all-round happiness that ripens in the present, so this month truly promises to be a joyful time for the Horse.

Work & Career - *Promotion luck*

A good time to look ahead at your career path before you. There is promotion luck on the cards with an increase in salary. Don't worry about the amount of your pay raise. Instead, focus on the honour of being elevated. Your promotion will come with greater responsibilities, but you are happy taking them on. Get to know your colleagues better. There may be one or two who may not be entirely happy for you as you move up the career ladder, but you can easily win them over if you turn on the charm. Don't respond to envious reactions by those in competition with you; instead, work at becoming their friend. They could end up becoming your biggest allies.

Business - *Something big coming*

You may experience a massive capital inflow this month. Sales exceed expectations, or at least meet them, so all is well in the foreseeable future. Even better, old debts you had almost given up on can be collected! So this becomes a bonus. Maintain close ties with those you work with, as they will stand you in good stead. Something good is coming your way and it is more than one surprise. So get ready for a few pleasant surprises! Perhaps an unexpected visit from someone you lost contact with, profitable offers, great bargains or one-off gifts. And you don't even have to lift a finger to make all this happen!

This is the time to try new things and take on new approaches. Your personal luck is strong so you can take risks, as so much is stacked in your favour.

Love & Relationships - *Long-term happiness*
You can take your relationship to the next level as this is the time when love luck is strongest. If you want to get married, declare your intentions. If reciprocated, you can start making plans! And if not, at least you know so you don't waste any more time. Whatever your situation, you are in a good place. Those who have reached the end of the road in a relationship can leave and start again, feeling positive. Chances are, if you are in that kind of situation, you already have someone else in mind. If you don't, you soon will!

Education - *Competitive*
You are highly motivated and achieve much scholarly success. Since studies come easy now, you should put in even more effort as the results are multiplied manifold! A little more effort now will prove so worthwhile later. Always exploit such a situation when a little investment brings returns that are out of proportion to your input.

ENHANCER FOR THE MONTH: Place the **6 Birds Auspicious Multiplier** in the South. Your big break could come this month.
For wealth, keep the **Asset Wealth Bull** within easy visibility in the home, in the West, or in the South.

12th Month
Jan 6th - Feb 3rd 2022

BETRAYAL STAR WARNS YOU OF FALSE FRIENDS

As the year swings from Rat to Ox year, the Betrayal Star makes a temporary appearance, warning you to be careful of traitors in your midst. They cannot do you real harm but may hurt you emotionally. Steel yourself for this kind of disappointment and you won't get hurt. There is also risk of money loss, theft and cheating, so don't trust others too easily. Avoid taking big risks in business and in the stock market. The #7 can also be a violent star, so it is best to be extra vigilant. Ladies, don't stay out too late at night. Be careful of petty robbers, but also of unsavoury characters who can take advantage if given the chance. Don't drink too much, only party with people you trust, watch your drink doesn't get spiked.

....

Work & Career - *Watch what you say*
You seem prickly and others sense you are being difficult. Don't be easily provoked as you will be falling into a trap. Search for friends in your midst as you will need their support. Those with a strong ally base at work will fare better. Get close to colleagues but don't

reveal secrets. Some things are best kept close to your chest. Certain opinions you have of others that are not flattering should not be bandied about. Keep tight-lipped else you could be making unnecessary enemies. Some upcoming business that seems cumbersome can be a blessing in disguise, so brace yourself for this possibility. Since your stars are not shining brightly, do all the right things; arrive on time to work, don't be late for meetings, submit proposals with relevant documents. Any form of slackness will be noticed and could count against you.

Business - *Mishaps*

An unproductive month made worse by minor mishaps. You spend most of the time putting out fires instead of getting on with business. Things go wrong due to circumstances beyond your control. You can also be cheated out of money from previous investments or current ones by some sweet talker. Don't enter into new partnerships now as you could be taken advantage of. However, your company can grow from within. Make use of existing resources. Focus on quality and keep track of your expenses. Make sure all accounts are in order and no one is pulling a fast one on you!

Avoid speculating, gambling and any form of risk-taking this month. Good idea to carry some form of protection.

Love & Relationships - *Take things slow*

Your big ideals about relationships don't always match up when it comes to reality. You may find yourself attracted to someone with an aggressive nature, then resent it when they try to control you. Be harsh with yourself - if your find yourself in a relationship you know has no future, better call it quits now. If still single, take things slow. Not the best time to go steady. Nothing is quite as it seems, so better to wait till the energies are more settled if you want to turn things up a notch.

Home & Family - *Beware Robbery Star*

Your priority should be security. Protect yourself against the Robbery Star by investing in an alarm system if you have to. Don't take safety for granted. Have the **Door Guardians Plaque** in the NW and a **Blue Rhino and Elephant** near your front door.

Education - *Parental guidance*

The young Horse may feel a strong need to take charge. But when you're too headstrong, you make mistakes. And when you do, it's best to admit them rather than sweep everything under the carpet. While you want to make your own decisions, you could always do with some good advice from your parents. They can see things you can't.

CURE FOR THE MONTH: Carry the **Anti-Cheating Amulet**. Ladies, carry the **Night Spot Protection Amulet**.

Night Spot Protection Amulet